Evaluating Service-Learning
Activities and Programs

David A. Payne

The Scarecrow Press, Inc.
Technomic Books
Lanham, Maryland, and London
2000

KH

SCARECROW PRESS, INC.
Technomic Books

Published in the United States of America
by Scarecrow Press, Inc.
4720 Boston Way, Lanham, Maryland 20706
http://www.scarecrowpress.com

4 Pleydell Gardens, Folkestone
Kent CT20 2DN, England

Copyright © 2000 by David A. Payne

British Library Cataloguing in Publication Information Available

Library of Congress Cataloging-in-Publication Data
Payne, David A.
    Evaluating service-learning activities and programs / David A. Payne.
        p. cm.
    Includes bibliographical references and index.
    ISBN 0-8108-3747-1 (alk. paper)
    1. Student service—United States—Evaluation—Case studies. 2. Student
service—United States—Planning—Case studies. I. Title.

LC220.5 .P39   2000
371.3—dc21

                                                                                00-020811

∞™The paper used in this publication meets the minimum requirements of
American National Standard for Information Sciences—Permanence of Paper
for Printed Library Materials, ANSI/NISO Z39.48—1992.
Manufactured in the United States of America.

11/22/04

Dedicated to

Polly and Allen, Jim and LaWayne, Parents of Distinction
and
Mi Tica, Beverly, Esposa Especial

If we do not lay out ourselves in the service of mankind whom should we serve?
— Abigail Adams, *Letter to John Thaxter*

And he gave it for his opinion, that whoever could make two ears of
corn or two blades of grass to grow upon a spot of ground where only one
grew before, would deserve better of mankind, and do more essential
service to his country, than the whole race of politicians put together.
— Jonathan Swift, *Gulliver's Travels*, 1726

Contents

List of Tables and Figures

Preface

As our good ship approached the lush island shores of Servicia, the natives rushed to their boats to welcome us. As was the ethic of the culture, their boats were made from recycled oil drums. Servicia is a small island nation but one that possesses powerful educational secrets. A small band of Servicians conquered Washington, D.C., in 1972 and coerced millions of dollars of tribute from the chiefs to support the development of their culture. They were quite friendly and brought trinkets made from pop-top can rings, popsicle sticks, beads, and old Elect Bill Clinton buttons. While wandering the nature paths we encountered their Orthodox temples of learning where youth are instructed daily to apply what they learn in the classroom to everyday life. There was even a museum that contained artifacts of a prehistoric culture: a mimeograph machine and a textbook. We learned that Margaret Mead had passed this way many decades ago, but she was not allowed to land because she couldn't pass PRAXIS. The inhabitants of this growing island are primarily from a tribe called Deweyites. Deweyites practice an ancient religion that practices "using of the hands" rituals, much to the chagrin of the Textites who do nothing but read. Everyone on the island is required to participate in Adopt-a-Stream and a Adopt-a-Highway programs.

Selected ecologically certified huts were given over to tutoring where the older inhabitants would pass on their cultural history to the youth. Their language has great poetic beauty and obscurity. Strong taboos are imposed on disagreement or any inhibition to sociability.

The intent of the foregoing allegory is to humorously symbolize the impact of service-learning on civilization as we know it. The service-learning "movement" grows stronger and more pervasive each year. The benefits, such as hands-on learning in a real-life context, fit well with many of today's educational and vocational (School-to-Work) needs. Not to be overlooked are the personal, moral, and ethical lessons that can be gleaned from a service-learning experience. Surely society will benefit greatly from the presence and participation of a more civilized populace.

As opposed to a great many educational innovations that tend to be treated as appendages to the curriculum, the service-learning philosophy and method are integrated into the ongoing educational program. As such they need to be evaluated at the same level as any instructional strategy. It is the intent of this volume to provide some ideas that will prove helpful in those evaluation efforts.

Curriculum evaluation is virtually a full-time task under the best of conditions. An attempt to isolate a particular aspect of the instructional program is perhaps impractical. Since service-learning is integrated into the ongoing program, evaluation can proceed as a matter of course. What is called for is a greater variety of methods. The following pages contain descriptions of procedures that experience, both historic and contemporary, have proven useful.

In terms of data use, my emphasis is on practical formative applications—how to improve the experience. There exist situations where summative evaluation might also be required. Provision has been made for these kinds of evaluations as well.

The primary audience for this book resides in the public schools, but the ideas and techniques could be generalized to any higher education setting. Common challenges are faced by representatives of both groups. Emphasis at the college and university level is typically more on the service component.

The evaluation field is vast and filled with extensive literature that is not readily available to those operating in the real world. I have attempted to provide a glimpse of the most readable and relevant documents and the required scholarly references by presenting a combined set of references and bibliography in end-of-chapter Referenceographies. I try to provide substantial treatment of only the most important topics without being too detailed, and I have drawn heavily on my earlier book, published by Kluwer, entitled *Designing Educational Project and Program Evaluations*.

Teachers, administrators, and evaluators (who may be one and the same), the audience for the book, have tremendous demands on their time. Little time is available to create new instrumentation for evaluation purposes. In addition to the instruments described throughout the book, an appendix containing new and used instruments is presented. The lineage of some of these instruments and their birth records have been lost. I apologize in advance for any possible lapse in attribution.

Following a general introduction to service-learning, this book is organized around the evaluation process, flowing from question formulation to instrumentation, collection, and application. Best current professional practice is emphasized and, I hope, presented in an efficient, easily digestible manner.

Chapters 2–8 each conclude with a case study. A true case study has been divided up to illustrate the ideas and procedures described in a particular chapter. A thought question is presented after the introductory material in each section of the case study. The reader is urged to reflect on the question and think through an answer to reinforce the ideas presented in the chapter. Case study materials drew heavily on the creativity of Marjo Baisden of the Wilkinson Public Schools in Irwinton, Georgia.

Many nurturing individuals have contributed to the creation of this volume. Primary of these is Janet Goetz whose nimble fingers and vast computer skills helped clarify my primitive hieroglyphics. Dick Grover of the Georgia State Department of Education has provided many opportunities to put ideas in the book into practice. He also read portions of the manuscript and made significant suggestions. Those in the real world of service-learning have contributed to my appreciation of the power of this instructional methodology. Among these are Gail Stewart, Carolyn Holland, Valerie Towler, Lynne Entrekin, and Barbara Rous. And, finally, I would like to thank the kids and teachers, bless 'em. They are what is exciting about education. Make no mistake, effective teaching is absolutely one of the hardest jobs in the world!

Many colleagues who are practicing evaluators have had positive influences on my thinking about evaluation. Among these are Mike McKenna of Georgia Southern University and Steve Cramer of the University of Georgia. Informative contributions were also made by Brian Hess. Dr. Mary Jo Brown helped develop my appreciation of the qualitative way of life; her influence is seen throughout the book.

One

What Is Service-Learning?

Mrs. Dean's fourth-grade class has discovered how much fun helping the local Humane Society can be. On Tuesdays and Thursdays they have special science units about domestic animals, and once a month they work at the society facility cleaning up, washing animals (with supervision), and putting together doggie bags. Once in a while they take a particularly gentle dog or cat to Pine Tree Manor, a local senior residence facility. It brings a lump to one's throat to see all that love between the residents and the animals. Three months ago, Chelsea, a black cocker spaniel, got to move into the Pines permanently. Kids talk about the animals and their new senior friends with everyone. It's amazing what they have learned about the breeding, development, and care of animals and how nutrition can help or hinder their growth.

At Beckwith Middle School the eighth grade has adopted neighboring Broadlands Elementary School first graders. Beckwith is right next door to the elementary school. Each student has a "reading buddy" and once a week they read to each other or together. Two years ago first graders' scores on the Iowa Tests of Basic Skills *(Form M) were below average, but results from this year's spring administration to the same children as third graders show an average gain of more than 15 percentile rank units in reading comprehension and 18 units in word analysis skills. Their eighth-grade tutors, who have now gone on to high school, have an average one-third unit higher grade point average than their peers.*

Beulah Rucker was a warm and caring African American lady who taught the children of slaves. After emancipation she started her own school. Over the years it grew, and in 1911 it became the private Beulah Rucker Industrial High School. Her home in Gainesville, Georgia, has become a significant southern historical site. The ravages of time unfortunately have taken their toll on her home. Students in Mr. Huberty's tenth-grade Georgia history class took on the project of restoration, repair, and beautification of this significant historic location. Their knowledge about their heritage has grown and has brought both local and out-of-town visitors.

Obviously these projects/activities share two components: academics and service. The linking of the two components makes for a powerful educational experience. Such powerful educational experiences can assist in bringing about educational reform.

Service-learning is not a new idea, but it is an idea whose time has come. In our society, which continues to develop and diversify, there exists a need to enhance both learning and the values that promote a stable society and individual adjustment. Service-learning is being systemized into our schools. It is hoped that, once experienced and internalized, the service concept will become a lifelong commitment to volunteerism.

But what is service-learning?

Service-Learning Defined

A May 1993 publication entitled *Alliance for Service-Learning in Education Reform* (ASLER) *Standards of Quality for School-Based Service-Learning* contains the following definition: "Service-learning is a method of teaching through which students apply newly acquired academic skills and knowledge to address real-life needs in their own communities." A very important dimension of the service-learning experience is that it deals with real-life needs. One frequently heard criticism of today's public education efforts is that they are not relevant to contemporary problems. Service-learning, with its community orientation, is one way to help build in that desired relevance. In addition, by having a "real-life" orientation, service-learning is more likely to motivate and generate learner enthusiasm than more traditional text-based approaches. Service-learning provides experiences that

- meet actual community needs;
- are coordinated in collaboration with the school and community;
- are integrated into each young person's academic curriculum;
- provide structured time for a young person to think, talk, and write about what he/she did and saw during the actual service activity;
- provide young people with opportunities to use newly acquired academic skills and knowledge in real-life situations in their own communities;
- enhance what is taught in the school by extending student learning beyond the classroom; and
- help to foster a sense of caring for others and civic responsibility.

Students are the focus of our efforts to bring about change. If a program were able to meet these expectations what might be the impact on students?

Anticipated Student Outcomes from Service-Learning

In a 1996 publication the National Association of Partners in Education listed the following hoped-for changes in students. Service-learning activities should create an environment where students can:

- improve their communication skills
- enhance their self-esteem
- acquire job skills
- enhance applications of learning
- improve school attendance and behavior
- improve their grades and test scores
- create enriched environment for partnerships
- improve school-community relations
- experience ownership in a project or activity
- better understand the responsibility of citizenship

- improve their problem-solving skills
- acquire project-specific skills
- acquire academic skills
- address community needs
- enhance school spirit and pride
- improve their team-building skills
- develop leadership skills
- increase student motivation
- improve their retention of knowledge and skills

What Research Tells Us

Do good things happen when students are engaged in service-learning? There is evidence at the public school level that being involved just one hour or more a week can significantly reduce at-risk behavior. Although one cannot argue cause and effect, Benson (1993) suggests the positive influence of service-learning on at-risk behavior for 6th–12th graders in table 1.1 (percent reporting):

Table 1.1 Student Benefits from Service-Learning Experiences

Behavior	Service-Learning Participants	Non-Participants
Binge Drinking	18%	30%
Problem Drug Use	9%	18%
Daily Cigarette Use	9%	18%
Frequent Alcohol Use	7%	14%
Vandalism	7%	13%
Skipping School	7%	13%

Not only are the benefits of service-learning and volunteerism seen in the schools, their impact is also evident in business and industry. A study of corporate volunteerism conducted by General Mills revealed the following benefits to the company and the employees:

- over one-half gained skills relevant to the workplace;
- over one-third gained skills relevant to their specific job;
- employee training and skills-building were supported;
- corporate team-building and interpersonal skills were enhanced;
- opportunities for people from different divisions of the company to interact were created;
- links between company and community improved;
- company's public image was enhanced;
- 98 percent of employees support the company's commitment to volunteerism;
- 65 percent of employees gained skills they can use outside of work;
- 91 percent of employees gained a better understanding of the community in which they live; and
- 93 percent of employees found satisfaction in their experience.

Recent compelling evidence about the positive impact of service-learning programs and projects comes from a national study sponsored by the Corporation for National Service and conducted by the Center for Human Resources of Brandeis University and Abt Associates (Melchior, 1997). Among many positive, statistically significant findings were a meaningful impact on measures of civic attitudes, such as those of social responsibility, acceptance of cultural diversity, and service leadership (defined as the degree to which students feel they are aware of needs in a community, are able to develop and implement a service project, and are committed to service now and later in life). In addition, program participants scored statistically higher on school grades (math, social studies, and science), core grade point average (average of English, math, science, and social studies), and educational aspiration (wanting to graduate from a four-year college). There is strong evidence indeed that participation in service-learning programs makes a difference.

At the higher education level, Markus, Howard, and King (1993) have reported that students in a large undergraduate political science course where service-learning was a major component were more likely (than a control "no-service" group) to report that they had (a) applied principles from the course to new situations, (b) performed up to their potential, and (c) significantly increased their awareness of societal problems. In this situation service-learning took the forms of twenty hours of service opportunities in a homeless shelter, women's crisis center, or ecology center or tutoring at-risk primary or high school students. Course grades were also statistically significantly higher than those of contrast students.

It can be seen that both formal and informal data strongly support the utility of the service-learning method as an instructional approach. In a sense it is an optimal technique as it yields both learning (cognitive) and attitudinal (affective) benefits.

Rationale for Service-Learning

By harkening back to educational psychologist John Dewey (1916) we can find a foundation for service-learning. His philosophy of education was based on the necessary relationship of knowledge and action, the so-called learn by doing principal. The likelihood of faster and more permanent learning was enhanced if "education" took place in and with a realistic task environment and if it was accompanied by the sharing of experiences. Less well appreciated is the fact that Dewey also professed to support character education in the same context, that is, to truly learn to be a responsible individual one must act like one. So practice makes . . . well you get the idea.

A takeoff on Dewey's ideas is embodied in the notion of the Cone of Experience (figure 1.1). The illustration of these ideas simply underscores the importance of experience in the support of learning, be it academic, ethical, or moral. With students actively involved in the classroom and the community, learning and character development should follow.

Contemporary educational psychologists have drawn upon Dewey's ideas and the research and observations of Piaget to create a learning theory called **social constructivism** (Orlich, Harder, Callahan, and Gibson, 1998). This view of learning generally holds that students should be active learners who construct knowledge out of personal experiences. Knowledge does not exist outside the student, as objectivists claim, but is molded, modified, and expanded by students depending on their experiences. The tenets of modern social constructivism are summarized in figure 1.2 on page 8.

The fit with the service-learning instructional approach seems quite natural. The student is actively involved and shares experiences with classmates. The philosophy works equally well for both the academic and service components of the experience. The role of the teacher is as facilitator, but not as sole authority because they are partners. The teacher guides and supports learners' own construction of knowledge with concrete and realistic examples and experiences. Such an instructional experience must be more palatable to the student than being spoon-fed information in a predetermined form. How much more meaningful for a student to "learn" science concepts by a real-life experience in a local stream than trying to memorize a variety of facts and concepts. Service-learning lives so that students may learn.

Developing a Service-Learning Program

It is not the intent of this brief section, or this book for that matter, to address in detail the development of a service-learning program. Some general perspectives on the usual steps in the process will be discussed, however. A process developed by the National Association of Partners in Education (1994) is adapted here to exemplify the usual approach. Although presented here in "linear" form, a program usually evolves out of a desire to implement a service-learning program with a lot of things happening simultaneously. That desire might originate from a felt or observed need or might come from institutional pressure.

Beginning with an **awareness** of the need for change on the part of teachers, the school, or students, the first thing to happen might be to:

■ **Conduct a Formal Needs Assessment**
Answers to the general question, "What are the needs or areas of concern or interest whereby educational efforts could be coupled with service activities to contribute to the

Figure 1.1   Cone of Experience

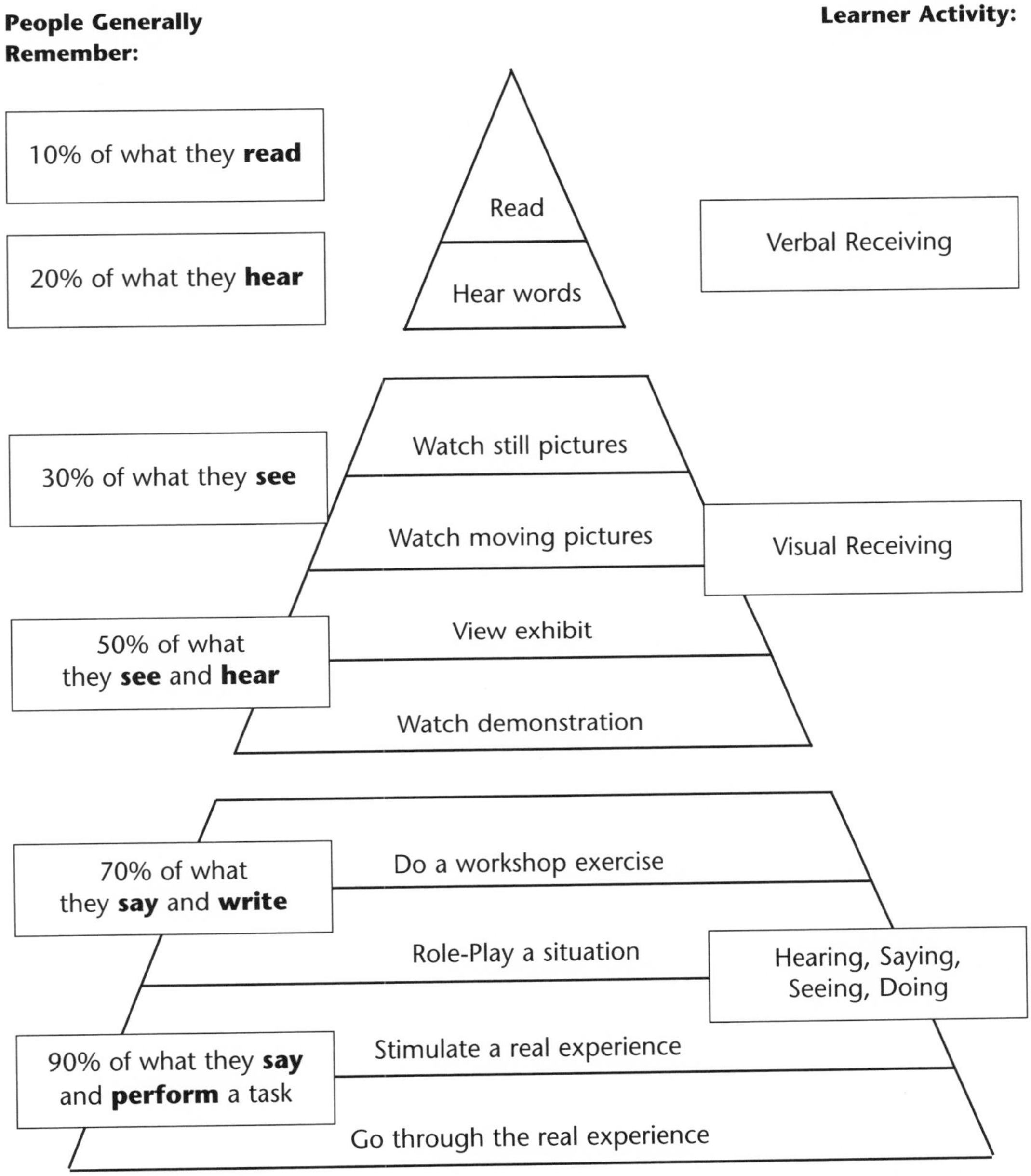

**People Generally
Remember:**   **Learner Activity:**

10% of what they **read**	Read	Verbal Receiving
20% of what they **hear**	Hear words	
30% of what they **see**	Watch still pictures	
	Watch moving pictures	Visual Receiving
50% of what they **see** and **hear**	View exhibit	
	Watch demonstration	
70% of what they **say** and **write**	Do a workshop exercise	
	Role-Play a situation	Hearing, Saying, Seeing, Doing
90% of what they **say** and **perform** a task	Stimulate a real experience	
	Go through the real experience	

community?" Community here is broadly defined to include the school, other classes, public or private agencies, community organizations, or the public in general. Representatives may search existing archival data, conduct surveys or interviews (e.g., focus groups), or simply **listen** to society members talking among themselves to identify targets. What is sought is a place where the interests of the school, community, and potential partners have a common focus. By involving students in the process at the beginning, during project identification and selection, ownership is significantly enhanced. Next, they might:

Figure 1.2   Tenets of Modern Social Constructivism

- Learning is dependent on the prior conceptions the learner brings to the experience.
- The learner must construct his or her own meaning.
- Learning is contextual.
- Learning is dependent on the shared understandings learners negotiate with others.
- Effective teaching involves understanding students' existing cognitive structures and providing appropriate learning activities to assist them.
- Teachers can use one or more key strategies to facilitate conceptual change, depending on the congruence of the concepts with student understanding and conceptualization.
- The key elements of conceptual change can be addressed by specific teaching methods.
- Greater emphasis should be placed on "learning how to learn" than on accumulating facts. In terms of content, less is more.

After Anderson et al., 1994.

■ Identify Potential Resources

Potential resources might be any people, materials, equipment, and funding available from a school, district, the general community, and businesses to help meet identified needs. Categories of resources might include the school, colleges and universities, community agencies, businesses, and state, federal, and local government agencies. Then:

■ Specify Goals and Objectives

Broad statements of intent should lead to a more specific measurable operationalization of expected outcomes. For example:

> *Goal:* Students will enhance their knowledge about science as a result of participating in the Adopt-A-Creek project, which will improve the quality of community environment.
>
> *Objective:* Students will learn three major facts about water pollution by the end of the first week of the Adopt-a-Creek project.

Usually the intended outcomes of a service-learning project include mention of the audience or target, expected behavioral change, and context within which the activity will take place. The range of content considered in service-learning projects is virtually limitless.

Content of Service-Learning Projects

The content of service-learning projects is limited only by the imagination and creativity of the participants. The limits are boundless, as illustrated in figure 1.3, which lists areas for potential projects from the service-learning programs in South Carolina.

Figure 1.3   Categories of Service-Learning Projects

Education

School Readiness
- Child care
- Head Start/preschool
- Family literacy

School Success
- In-class support
- After-school tutoring
- After-school mentoring
- After-school assistance

Public Safety

Crime Prevention
- Violence prevention patrols
- Conflict resolution/ community mediation
- Reduction of substance abuse
- After-school activities

Crime Control
- Community policing
- Victim assistance
- Anti-victimization programs
- Juvenile justice programs

Human Needs

Health
- Independent living assistance
- Supporting community health clinics
- Prenatal care
- Health care for families or young children
- Hospitals/nursing homes

Home
- Shelter support for the homeless
- Rehabilitating low-income housing
- Public assistance transition support
- Assistance to senior citizens

Environment

Neighborhood Environment
- Revitalizing neighborhoods/school grounds
- Eliminating environmental risks
- Energy efficiency efforts
- Recycling

Natural Environment
- Conserving and restoring public lands
- Trail maintenance
- Natural resource sampling, mapping, and monitoring
- Community gardens
- Air and water quality
- Reforestation

■ **Design Programs/Projects**

The usual design for a service-learning activity results in an overall plan that includes one or more lesson plans to forge the academic link. All relevant partners to the service-learning project should help with the program design; students, teachers, administrators, business and community volunteers/partners. A typical service-learning lesson plan will include:

- a statement of student goals;
- a statement of needed resources;
- description of the preparation needed for the activity;
- specification of the nature of the service activity;
- explanation of how students (and partners) will "reflect" on experience;
- explanation of ways in which students' contributions and successes will be recognized; and
- description of methods to be used to monitor and evaluate experience.

Student ownership (and that of the teacher, too) is increased by involving everyone at the design stage. A very important step is to:

■ Recruit Participants

Once the obvious advantages and benefits of service-learning are explained to the community and school, enthusiastic buy-in will take place. Community members really do want to be involved in the schools, they just need an opportunity. Clear expectations of all participants need to be specified. Don't overlook an extremely large (and growing) pool of volunteers—senior citizens. The partnerships formed and nurtured will be long-lasting. No matter how great they are, you will still have to:

■ Organize and Train Participants

Whether coming from the school or community, participants will need orientation, sometimes training, and assignment. Volunteers do have rights concerning suitable placement and some realistic choice about the nature and extent of participation. Students' needs must be considered. The whole issue of required versus voluntary student participation will need to be addressed.

The mentor of a service-learning project must be aware that it will be ever-changing. As the project matures and students become accustomed to and expand their roles, the project and activities will evolve. In particular, greater student leadership will be exhibited. Be sure to have a plan to:

■ Monitor and Evaluate

Finally to the point of this book: How will the service-learning experience be evaluated? Monitoring (sometimes called **formative evaluation**) will take place during the development and implementation phases, and summative evaluation at the conclusion. A variety of data types and sources will be used. Both academic and service components will need to be addressed. See chapter 2 for a more detailed treatment of the process.

Major Components of Service-Learning Programs

The general framework for developing, conducting, and implementing a service-learning program includes (Duckenfield & Swanson, 1992):

Preparation, which consists of the learning activities that take place prior to the service itself. Prior to their service experience, students must understand what is expected of them as well as what they can expect from the service project. Preparation components include the following:

- identifying and analyzing the problem
- training and orientation
- selecting and planning the project

Action corresponds to the service itself and needs to met certain criteria. It must:

- be meaningful
- have academic integrity
- have adequate supervision

- provide for student ownership
- be developmentally appropriate

Reflection then enables students to critically think about their service experience. When students reflect on their experiences, they think about them, share them with others, and learn from them. The reflection time is a structured opportunity for students to learn from their experiences. They can reflect through:

- discussion
- reading
- writing

- projects
- the arts
- presentations

Reflection also provides an important opportunity to refine academic skills.

Celebration is the final component of service-learning; it recognizes students for their contributions and provides closure. Society needs to let young people know that their contributions are valued. There are many ways that this final component of service-learning can be implemented, including:

- school assemblies
- certificates
- special media coverage

- pizza parties
- joint celebration with service recipients

All components must be present for the experience to work. This is where student ownership is exhibited and reinforced.

The Role of Evaluation in the Process

There are, unfortunately, many school personnel who feel that evaluation is a plague. Fear, threat, and anxiety surround some of the evaluations that take place in and around our schools. We know that we cannot do a professional job if we do not evaluate students, but what about evaluating ourselves and our programs? Well-conceived evaluation programs can add a great deal of relevant information to the data needed for treating the ills of education and making rational educational decisions (and we need lots of those). Effective and efficient prescriptions are often difficult to find, and, like health care in general, can be costly.

The best approach to evaluation-is to involve *all* relevant stakeholders at *every* stage of the process (preparation, action, reflection, and celebration). Evaluation activities need to be planned and implemented. Participants can reflect on what has happened, is happening, and will happen. Finally, the results can become part of the culminating service-learning celebration. No better environment could be created in which to share the good things that have happened, and that includes evaluation results.

Standards for Effective Service-Learning Programs

But what constitutes a good and effective service-learning program? Members of the Alliance for Service-Learning in Education Reform (ASLER) in 1995 explicated Standards of Quality for School-Based and Community-Based Service-Learning. They are:

- Effective service-learning efforts strengthen service and academic learning.
- Model service-learning provides concrete opportunities for youth to learn new skills, to think critically, and to test new roles in an environment that encourages risk-taking and rewards competence.
- Preparation and reflection are essential elements in service-learning.
- Youths' efforts are recognized by those served, including their peers, the school, and the community.

- Youth are involved in the planning.
- The service students perform makes a meaningful contribution to the community.
- Effective service-learning integrates systematic formative and summative evaluation.
- Service-learning connects the school or sponsoring organization and its community in new and positive ways.
- Service-learning is understood and supported as an integral element in the life of a school or sponsoring organization and its community.
- Skilled adult guidance and supervision are essential to the success of service-learning.
- Preservice training, orientation, and staff development that include the philosophy and methodology of service-learning best ensure that program quality and continuity are maintained.

Drawing on these ideas and now many years of experience the National Service-Learning Cooperative of the National Youth Leadership Council (1998) has synthesized the critical elements of an effective service-learning program as follows (in paraphrased form):

Effective Service-Learning Activities
Learning Outcomes
1. Establish clear educational goals that require the application of concepts, content, and skills from the academic disciplines and involve students in the construction of their own knowledge.
2. Engage students in tasks that challenge them cognitively and developmentally.
3. Use assessment to enhance student learning and to document and evaluate how well students have met content and skills standards.

Service Outcomes
4. Engage students in service activities that have clear goals, meet genuine needs in the school and community, and have significant consequences for themselves and others.
5. Employ systematic formative and summative evaluation for the improvement of the service experience.

Support Structure
6. Involve the student in selecting, designing, implementing, and evaluating the service activity.
7. Reflect diversity of participants, practices, and outcomes.
8. Promote communication, interaction, and collaboration in the community and with partners.
9. Prepare students to understand the nature of the task, their role, required skills, safety requirements, and interpersonal dimensions of the service activity.
10. Employ student reflection before, during, and after the service experience, and as a central element in fulfilling curriculum objectives.
11. Engage students in multiple celebration activities to validate service work.

That's a tall order. What would a "typical" service-learning project look like?

Illustrative Service-Learning Projects

The parents, teachers, and students of Whitesville Road Elementary School in LaGrange, Georgia, working with Dr. Michael McKenna of Georgia Southern University, have created the following design for a service-learning project.

Sample Third Grade Service-Learning Activity

Environmental Focus:
Reduce, Reuse, Recycle

Academic Link:
Science, Language Arts, Reading, Math, Art, Social Studies

Level:
Third Grade

Student Goals:
- The student will identify the need for packaging and how packaging can reduce the amount of food waste that goes to a landfill.
- The student will be able to recognize that reuse is a viable option for extending the life of a product.
- The student will demonstrate an understanding of the proper procedures for storage, and preparation for recyclables.

Personnel Needed:
Students, teachers, administrators, business partners, county Clean and Beautiful representative, recycling center representative.

Resources Needed:
- Recycling collection bins
- Information books and videotapes on reduction, recycling, and reuse
- school map, scale, calculators, child's wagon, durable trash bags.

Preparation for Service Activity:
Teachers will obtain free literature/supplies from civic organizations. Students will research the benefits of reducing, reusing, and recycling. They will calculate the anticipated revenue from the recycling project. The staff will also inform the staff and students in other classes of the environmental and financial benefits of the project.

Service Activity:
Students will begin a school and home recycling campaign and donate any money earned from the campaign to purchase Accelerated Reader books for the school.

Reflection:
Students will conduct a project on reusing old tires to make a flower garden on our school campus. Students will write articles and put them on our Web page reporting on their experiences, what they learned, and the impact of their project on the community.

Celebration:
The students will go to the recycling center and to the landfill. To celebrate the addition of new books to the media center through the money earned from recycling, students will be invited to enjoy a storytelling activity in the media center.

Monitoring/Evaluation:
Data from the recycling effort will be used in math classes to apply computational and graphing concepts. Writing samples will be analyzed for communication effectiveness using a collaboratively created teacher rubric. Content analyses of two six-person focus groups will be undertaken at the end of the project year. A fifteen-item service-learning experience opinionnaire will be administered to all students. School discipline data will be collected and contrasted with archival data.

Estimated Date for Completion:
Project will begin at the opening of the school year and continue throughout the year.

The following class project was contributed by Lori J. Bearden of Bascomb Elementary School in Woodstock, Georgia, and her students. It was a winner and well received.

Sample Fifth Grade Service-Learning Activity
(Quilt for Homeless Shelter)

Student Goals:
- Improve their awareness of early American transportation and westward movement
- Improve ability to make inferences in stories
- Improve comprehension skills
- Improve ability to apply learned math skills
- Discover the time factors faced by early Americans in everyday task

Writing Skills:
- Persuasive essays

Math:
- Students are given the dimensions of the quilt, how many squares, and how large the borders will be. They figure the size of each square.

Home Economics:
- Sewing, appliqué

Economics:
- How has the value of quilts changed over the years? Why?

Language Arts:
- Persuasive essays

Communication–Debate Question:
To whom will the quilt be donated?
- homeless people
- women's shelter
- tornado victims
- children's advocacy center
- nursing home

Resources Needed:
Story "Grandma Essie's Covered Wagon" or "The Josefina Story Quilt"
- fabric scraps
- needles, thread, embroidery yarn
- batting
- parent volunteers

Preparation for Service Activity:
Students read "Grandma Essie's Covered Wagon" following a social studies unit on Early American Transportation/Westward Movement. Students make inferences on family displacement. Students discuss struggles of early families (compare Social Studies and Language Arts versions). Students predict time needed to make a quilt. Students calculate quilt size, and design and make squares and quilt (after parents piece together the squares). Life journeys are discussed.

Service Activity:
Students prepare persuasive essays to debate about who will receive the quilt. Following the debate, the students decide to donate the quilt to the homeless shelter.

Reflection:
Before we send the quilt, students write a journal entry about their contribution to the quilt. Class discusses our entries and how it feels to part with the quilt. Prediction! What journey might our quilt make?

Celebration:
- Picture of class with quilt reproduced, one for each service-learning folder and for school newsletter and local newspaper
- Presentation of quilt to homeless shelter representatives

Evaluation:
- Short objective test on early American transportation and westward movement
- Develop scoring rubric or use state rubric for essays
- Brief (three to four questions) survey of student feelings about what creating and giving quilt meant to them
- Brief survey (or interview) of homeless shelter staff about acceptance and use of quilt

Partners:
Local Ministries and Homeless Shelter

Note in both of these projects the integration of many different academic skills!

Conclusion

The implementation of service-learning programs in the schools helps to give back to the community a sense of ownership and investment in the schools. It also has great public relations value for partners (nonprofit or for-profit), and perhaps even financial incentives for business partners. Business partners will be involved in preparing future workers who have a more realistic and hands-on orientation to the world of work. The whole school-to-work transition is facilitated by a greater sense of responsibility. Let us not forget, finally, the smiles of satisfaction on the faces and the enthusiasm exhibited by the learner-servers!

What about the future? Educational practitioners and researchers are urged to undertake some basic investigations of the factors that contribute to the success of the service-learning methodology. Under what conditions are the effects maximized? What kinds of students tend to benefit most from the service experience? What are the best ways to incorporate the method into the curriculum? What teaching styles and learning styles tend to yield the best results? Finally, we need systematic follow-up studies of both the academic and citizenship consequences of the service-learning experience.

Referenceography

Anderson, R. D., et al. (1994). *Issues of curriculum reform in science, mathematics and higher order thinking across the disciplines.* Washington, DC: U.S. Department of Education, Office of Research, OR 94-3408.

Benson, P. L. (1993). *The troubled journey.* Minneapolis: Search Institute.

Billig, S. H., & Kraft, N. P. (1996). Linking Title I and service-learning. Denver: RMC Research Corporation.

Conrad, D., & Hedin, D. (1991). School-based community service: What we know from research and theory. *Phi Delta Kappan*, 72(10), 743–749.

DeVitis, J. L., Johns, R. W., & Simpson, D. J. (1998). *To serve and learn (The spirit of community in liberal education)*. New York: Peter Lang.

Dewey, J. (1916). *Democracy and education*. New York: The Free Press.

Duckenfield, M., & Swanson, L. (1992). *Service-learning: Meeting the needs of youth*. Clemson, SC: National Dropout Prevention Center, Clemson University.

Erickson, J. A., & Anderson, J. B. (1997). *Learning with the community*. Washington, DC: American Association for Higher Education.

Hedin, D., & Conrad, D. (1990). Learning from service experience: Experience is the best teacher or is it? In *Combining service and learning: A resource book for community service*. Raleigh, NC: NSIEE.

Jacoby, B., & Associates (1996). *Service-learning in higher education*. San Francisco: Jossey- Bass.

Markus, G. B., Howard, J. P. F., & King, D. C. (1993). Integrating community service and classroom instruction enhances learning: Results from an experiment. *Educational Evaluation and Policy Analysis* 15(4), 410–419.

Melchior, A. (1997). *National evaluation of learn and serve American school and community-based programs-Interim report*. Waltham, MA: Center for Human Resources, Brandeis University.

National Association of Partners in Education, Inc. (1994). *Service-learning & business/education partnerships-A guide for service-learning coordinators* (Second Revision, 1996). Alexandria, VA: National Association of Partners in Education.

National Service-Learning Cooperative (1998). *Essential elements of service-learning*. St. Paul, MN: National Youth Leadership Council.

Neal, M., Shumer, R., & Gorak, K. S. (1994). *Evaluation: The key to improving service-learning programs*. Minneapolis: Center for Experiential and Service-Learning, University of Minnesota.

Orlich, D. C., Harder, R. J., Callahan, R. C., & Gibson, H. W. (1998). *Teaching strategies—A guide to better instruction*. Boston: Houghton Mifflin.

Schine, J. (Ed.) (1997). *Service-learning* (Ninety-sixth Yearbook of the National Society for the Study of Education). Chicago: University of Chicago Press.

Schukar, R., Johnson, J., & Singleton, L. R. (1996). *Service-learning in the middle school curriculum: A resource book*. Boulder: Social Science Education Consortium.

South Carolina Department of Education (1994). *Serving to learn-High school manual*. Columbia: South Carolina Department of Education.

Two

The Need to Ask Evaluation Questions

It has been recorded that the first instance of evaluation took place in the Garden of Eden, and involved man, woman, an apple, and a serpent. Apparently, the program objectives were not being met. This was an illustration of an individual evaluation. At the publicly sponsored program level, perhaps the first recorded example was the evaluation that Pharaoh undertook of the ratio of costs to benefits when using Jewish laborers. Despite these horrific precedents, we continue to evaluate.

The world thirsts for knowledge and information. Such information can be used to better serve the public, build a better computer or mousetrap, or educate our youth. A bottom-line question, however, is How well are we doing these things? To find out we evaluate and monitor. People are always evaluating. We do it every day. We buy clothing, a car, or refrigerator. We select a movie or subscribe to a magazine. All these decisions require data-based value-judgments. Data take many forms. Sometimes we rely on our own experience or the opinions of others. Sometimes we require more formal information such as that derived from experiments and controlled studies. Educators make decisions about the effectiveness of curricula and/or programs, the progress of individual students toward specified goals, and the efficiency of instructional methods.

The most generally accepted definition of educational evaluation involves the idea of assessment of merit, or making judgments of value or worth. The process employs both quantitative and qualitative approaches. One theme of this book is that making informed value judgments about service-learning programs requires the availability of reliable and valid data, and the exercise of rational decision making. This is as true about programs, projects, and curricula as it is about individuals.

There are lots of fancy theories about how to do evaluations, but the basic process simply involves collecting, synthesizing, and making commonsense interpretations about the value of a project or experience.

The Context and Focus of Service-Learning Evaluation

The major activity that undergirds all evaluation activities is **documentation**. The dictionary definition of documentation is something like the systematic act of making the orderly presentation, organization, and communication of recorded special knowledge to produce a record of changes in variables.* Sounds like what we are after: special knowledge about how service-learning has changed the lives of students, teachers, parents, and community members. How will that documentation be used? The tree diagram in figure 2.1 should help us see the application.

The applications for **Accountability** purposes are pretty straightforward. The question asked is, Is what happened what was proposed to happen? This question may be in response to either a formal contract, where funding is involved, or an informal "curricular contract," where certain educational transactions are to take place. The goal of **Evaluation** has been defined as the assessment of merit or the judgment of value or worth. This can be accomplished with regard to:

- The worthwhileness of the activity itself (Value Status)
- The degree and adequacy to which procedures and processes were followed (Implementation Fidelity)
- The value of the impact of the activity or project (Impact)

*The American Heritage Dictionary, 1991, Boston: Houghton Mifflin Co.

Figure 2.1   Elements in the Documentation Process

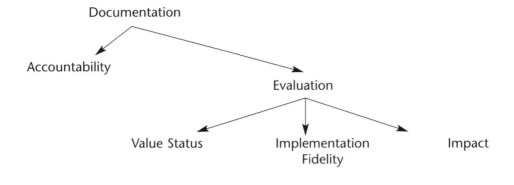

The Value Status category asks whether this is a worthwhile project or activity. It is evaluated in an absolute sense and usually before the fact in the sense that cooperative and collaborative decisions among stakeholders have led to the selection of the service-learning activity or program. Implementation (or monitoring) and Impact evaluation come very close to what traditionally have been called summative and formative evaluation, respectively.

In addition to the obvious need to evaluate service-learning activities for purposes of accountability and improvement, evaluation presents an opportunity for **reflection** (Hedin & Conrad, 1990; Neal, Shumer, & Gorak, 1994). Looking back over the service-learning activity or project provides insight into both the mechanics and operation of the process as well as its meaningfulness. If all stakeholders are involved in the evaluation, an opportunity to share and bond is also present. Stakeholders include not just students and school staff but partners and interested community members. Bringing together all interested parties during the "reflective" evaluation time also underscores the importance of the evaluation effort itself. Better data should result as should a more meaningful interpretation of the results. This valuable time can be used for planning and celebration, as well.

Summative and Formative Evaluation

Depending on the role the value judgments are to play, evaluation data may be used developmentally or to summarize. In the case of an overall decision, the role of evaluation is summative. An end-of-course assessment would be considered summative. Summative evaluation may employ absolute or comparative standards and judgments.

Formative evaluation, on the other hand, is almost exclusively aimed at improving an educational experience or product during its developmental phases and to monitor its implementation. A key element in the formative technique is feedback. Information is gathered during the developmental phase with an eye toward improving the total product or process.

With regard to the evaluation of service-learning activities and projects, the most important application is formative. We are interested in maximizing the benefit to both student and community. Frequent collection and digestion of impact data is therefore required. The traditional kinds of evaluation designs such as pre-post don't provide sufficient and timely information so that the activities and delivery mechanism can be refined, remodeled, or reinforced.

The suggestion has been made that summative and formative evaluations differ *only* with respect to the time when they are undertaken in the service of the program or project development. There are, however, other dimensions along which these two roles of evaluation could be contrasted. A very informative and succinct summary has been created by Worthen, Sanders, and Fitzpatrick (1997) and is summarized in table 2.1.

Table 2.1 Differences between Summative and Formative Evaluation

Basis for Comparison	Formative Evaluation	Summative Evaluation
Purpose	To improve program	To certify program utility
Audience	Program administrators, staff, and participants	Potential consumer or funding agency
Who Should Do It	Internal evaluator	External evaluator
Major Characteristic	Timely, developmental	Convincing
Measures	Often informal variety of methods and sources	Valid/reliable
Frequency of Data Collection	Frequent	Limited
Sample Size	Often small	Usually large
Questions Asked	What is working? What needs to be improved? How can it be improved?	What results occur? With whom? Under what condition? With what training? At what cost?

From Program Evaluation: Alternative Approaches and Practical Guidelines, *2nd ed., by Worthen, Sanders, and Fitzpatrick. Copyright 1997, 1987 by Longman Publishers USA. Reprinted by permission of Addison-Wesley Educational Publishers, Inc.*

Most evaluations use both approaches. Obviously an end-of-year summative evaluation can be formative for the next year. As projects and programs mature, the amount of time devoted to the type of evaluation will shift, with movement from more formative to more summative.

Formative and summative evaluation activities can take place in the context of the classroom learning environment or the project or program as a whole. As shown in figure 2.2, the focus could be on academic outcomes or service outcomes. Finally, data could be collected from at least five major sources: students, teachers, administrators, parents, and community members.

The major category is, however, Focus—namely, Academic or Service. Emphasis may be placed on the classroom or a program throughout a school. In many instances aggregating data over classrooms can yield a program evaluation, but this assumes a high degree of comparability in objectives, implementation, and instructional methods. Sampling techniques can be used to gather data on the impact of service activities—e.g., random samplings of classrooms with an "altruism survey."

If these are the targets for questions, what is the process? There are lots of metaphors for the evaluation process, ranging from a *Consumer Report*'s approach to the judicial (judge and jury) to the anthropological.

Figure 2.2 Context for Evaluation of Service-Learning Programs

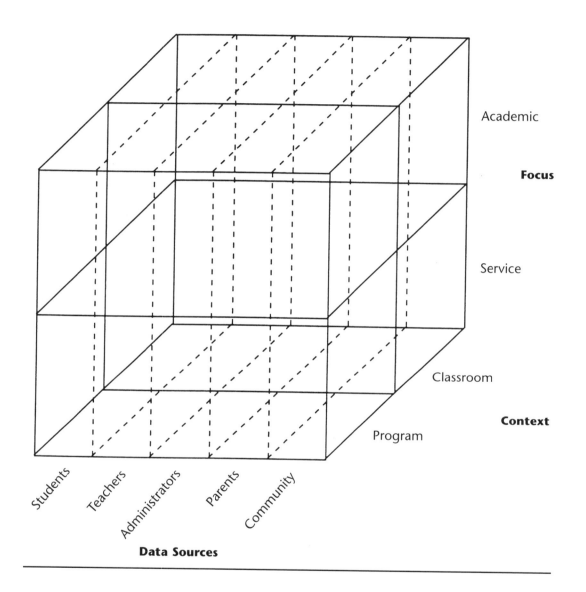

Steps in the Evaluation Process

There probably never will be total agreement on the nature of the activities and/or sequence of steps in the evaluation process. The kind of evaluation questions being asked, availability of resources, and time lines are some of the factors that would dictate the final form of the process. Basically, the process boils down, with some exceptions, to an application of the principles of the "objectives-based scientific method," *but not always being used in a linear fashion.* Some evaluations might simply require retrieval of information from records in files, while others might call for pilot or field studies. Such studies might be as simple and informal as sitting with a student and listening to him or her work through a new unit on long division, or it might be something as complex as a 20 percent sample achievement student survey study of all major physics objectives at the ninth-grade level.

Figure 2.3 illustrates the usual activities in conducting an evaluation. Only the major activities are identified. Information may be shared between blocks (activities/ processes), and decisions are continuously being modified and revised. The activities presuppose that a needs assessment has been conducted and that an innovative service-learning project or program has been proposed or put in place. The sequence of activities in figure 2.3 may be followed directly and exactly if summative evaluation is the role being played by evaluation, or periodically and systematically repeated if formative evaluation is the primary intent. At some point in the process all of the steps must be addressed—e.g., one has to deal somehow with objectives, or some kind of standards explicit or implicit will be brought to bear in interpretation. The sequence of activities may change depending on the requirements of the evaluation. It should be emphasized again that there is no temporal sequence implied except that goals for the project and evaluation questions generally come first.

All of the activities are important, but one of particular interest in developing a comprehensive evaluation program is Standard Setting. The specification of criteria may be the most important part of the evaluation process. The question asked is: On what basis do I make a value judgment? The criteria might relate to an individual (Did Karen learn 75 percent of today's vocabulary words about plants?) or group or institution (Did 80 percent of students in grade five in the county learn 80 percent of the capitals of 50 major countries?). We then gather data to evaluate the objectives. Standards may be set prior to data collection if the instrumentation is known or selected. It might take place after data collection but before decision making. One might specify an absolute level to be reached before agreeing that the objective had been mastered—e.g., 75 percent of the students must agree or strongly agree that their tutoring experience was rewarding, or some difference between service participants and nonparticipants might be specified—e.g., there will be at least a 15 percent difference in community volunteerism between high school students in the service-learning program and those who did not participate.

These steps have to be put into some meaningful framework.

A Dynamic Model for Evaluation—Naturalistic Inquiry

As noted, the steps in the evaluation discussed in the previous section are not locked rigidly in sequence. There is a flow of activity during the collection of information. It is a dynamic process, ever-changing, and evolving as new information is collected and perspectives gathered about implementation and progress.

The general model proposed for evaluating service-learning activities and projects is a modified naturalistic or anthropological approach. Naturalists have been described variously as scientists who investigate humanity and human culture. They examine strategies for living that are learned and shared by people or by members of living groups. They follow general procedures that involve (1) entering and establishing themselves in a community, (2) developing hypotheses, (3) collecting and synthesizing evidence, and (4) drawing conclusions. If one conceives of a classroom, school, or school system as a "culture," then the anthropological or naturalistic approach to investigation emerges as a metaphor for evaluation. Ethnography, being the documentation and description of social and cultural groups, is a method frequently used by service-learning evaluators.

Figure 2.3 Overview of Usual Steps in Evaluation Process

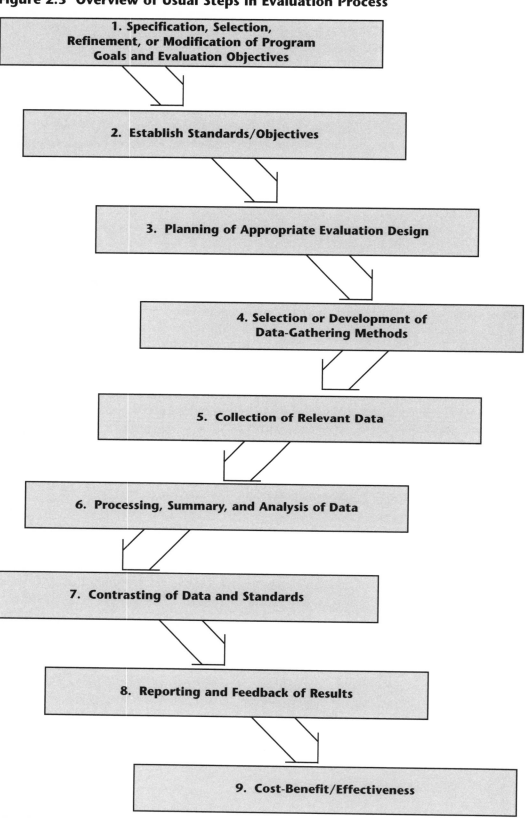

1. Specification, Selection, Refinement, or Modification of Program Goals and Evaluation Objectives

2. Establish Standards/Objectives

3. Planning of Appropriate Evaluation Design

4. Selection or Development of Data-Gathering Methods

5. Collection of Relevant Data

6. Processing, Summary, and Analysis of Data

7. Contrasting of Data and Standards

8. Reporting and Feedback of Results

9. Cost-Benefit/Effectiveness

After Payne, 1994.

Goals and objectives are still important. Activities (instruction) and projects need goals and objectives to help identify direction and intent. The evaluation of those "intents" and an assessment of their merit could be addressed directly by measuring them at the conclusion of an experience or by coming in the back door and seeing what objectives were in fact achieved. This back-door approach, sometimes called goal-free, does not begin with the rhetoric of the project, but rather focuses on what actually happened. There is an assumption that beginning from a goal or objectives base may result in tunnel vision for an evaluator. In addition to the increased likelihood of identifying unanticipated or side effects, goal-free evaluation also concerns itself with an assessment of the quality of program goals and objectives themselves. Obviously if goals or objectives are not worthwhile, their attainment is not meaningful.

The implication of the anthropological or naturalistic metaphor is perhaps not so much for the overall design of the evaluation as it is for the activities that occupy the evaluator's efforts and time. Patton (1987, p. 7), for example, notes that a qualitative/naturalistic evaluation would be concerned with:

- describing the program or project implementation in detail;
- analyzing program or project processes;
- describing participants and the nature of their participation;
- describing program impact cognitively, affectively, and behaviorally; and
- analyzing strengths and weaknesses of the program or project based on a variety of data and sources.

These general intents have been operationalized in the responsive evaluation approach advocated by Robert E. Stake (1975, 1983). Although likely to result in less measurement precision, the validity and usefulness of a responsive evaluation more than justifies its application. A responsive evaluator is concerned with producing a "product" or what Stake calls a **portrayal**. A portrayal is a verbally rich description of the program or project reflecting multiple realities that the evaluator has experienced. The key to gaining the data needed to generate a portrayal is the use of qualitative methods in naturally occurring situations. The closer the data are to the source in context, the more meaningful the judgments. Most experts expect the evaluator to make judgments of value, worth and merit, and not rely on some individual outside the environment to interpret the data. Among the methods a responsive/naturalistic/qualitative evaluator might use are: ethnography, case study, investigative journalism (another interesting metaphor), oral history, participant (interactive) or nonparticipant (noninteractive) observation, field study, or connoisseurship/criticism. As opposed to the quantitative (objectives-oriented) evaluator, a qualitative/responsive/naturalistic evaluator is likely to spend (1) less time in instrument development, (2) much more time observing the program or project and gathering judgments, and (3) much less time formally processing data, although sometimes qualitative data (such as those derived from observation, open-ended questionnaires, or interviews) will be subjected to extensive and time-consuming content analyses. The results of these analyses will sometimes be summarized with frequencies and percents for graphic display.

The advantages and disadvantages of the naturalistic/qualitative approach are summarized in table 2.2. A major appeal of the naturalistic/qualitative metaphor is the closeness of data (from observation) and interpretation (judgment of worth), thereby enhancing validity. When using structured paper-and-pencil devices, one frequently has the feeling that the leap from marks on the paper to "true" meaning is almost one of total faith. Qualitative methods tend to yield higher inference data—i.e., more subjectivity is involved in interpreting them. Do not overlook the loss of measurement precision that can also accompany the use of qualitative methods, however. The "human instrument" can be unpredictable and unreliable, but we need both qualitative and quantitative approaches. Mixed-method models have a lot to offer and can be compatible with naturalistic inquiry.

Table 2.2   Advantages and Disadvantages of Naturalistic Inquiry

Advantages	Disadvantages
1. Potentially greater validity	1. High degree of reliance on subjectivity
2. Greater responsiveness to stakeholders within context	2. Problems of reliability of human observers
3. Greater heuristic value and likelihood of new insights	3. Data collection and analysis likely to be labor-intensive
4. Encourages multiple data types and sources	4. Potentially very expensive
5. Less likely to miss unintended effects	
6. Nature of data is inherently credible and persuasive	
7. High degree of flexibility	
8. Emphasizes real and complex nature of evaluation context	

The Importance of Using Mixed Methods

The use of both qualitative and quantitative methods in an evaluation was emphasized in the previous section. Mixed-method designs have been defined as those that include at least one quantitative method and one qualitative method where neither method is inherently linked to a particular inquiry paradigm or philosophy (Caracelli & Greene, 1993). A mixed-method design using investigator triangulation (using a combination of methods in studying the same phenomena), where the evaluation team consists of both qualitative and quantitative evaluators committed to their inquiry paradigm and philosophy, is particularly strong. Evaluators bring extensive training, expertise, and experience in their particular paradigm and data collection approach to inform different aspects of the evaluation. It can be argued that different and important understandings can emerge by triangulating qualitative and quantitative evaluation methods using investigators who are strong in each approach.

In mixed-method designs, data from each method are analyzed independently and then points of agreement (confirmation) and disagreement (convergence) are sought. Quantitative data are numerical (but sometimes numerical for descriptive purposes) and are analyzed using a strategy such as constant comparative analysis or phenomenological analysis, which allows for emerging categories and relations among categories to be generated from participant data. There is no need to use strategies to artificially numerically code and transform rich narrative data into numerical form for analysis that would be comparable to quantitative data analysis. That undermines the basic reasons for conducting rigorous, in-depth qualitative evaluation. Analyzed and interpreted data from each approach are examined and compared by all evaluators to generate a broader understanding of the impact of the program being evaluated.

Evaluation Responsibility

Who is responsible for evaluating service-learning activities and programs? In chapter 1 we described an activity as a classroom experience; therefore, teachers have the primary obligation to assess the cognitive performance and/or affective impact of those tasks. If a decision has been made at the school or district (county) level to implement more extensive programs, some local coordinator or central office person will have monitored both implementation of the program and its evaluation. Service-learning is a philosophy of learning. As such, it permeates the curriculum. Its results could be evaluated repeatedly from the ongoing program or simply included as part of current curriculum evaluation efforts (Payne, 1974). The crucial element in the process is to make sure that the service-learning objectives are included in the classroom lesson plans and the local (or state) curriculum. Some of the instrumentation needed for service-learning evaluation already exists in the hands or minds of teachers, particularly that associated with performance and knowledge outcomes. Most of the "service" outcome measures have to be custom designed for the particular project. (See appendix C for ideas for such instruments.) Why do we continually assess and evaluate? To make more effective the teaching-learning process.

Once we have identified the steps and the general framework for the evaluation, how do we judge quality?

Program Standards and Criteria for Evaluation

Using criteria and standards can help produce a better evaluation plan and help judge how good a job we did in evaluating our service-learning activities. The following eleven criteria can be used to evaluate evaluation plans.

Scope:	Are all significant aspects of the program being addressed? (This obviously includes major activities and participants.)
Relevance:	Are all the data and information being collected appropriate to the evaluation questions? Will the information answer the questions we have raised for interested audiences?
Flexibility:	Is the evaluation plan open enough to accommodate changes in objectives, time lines, audiences, and data collection? (Since these evaluations take place in ongoing educational programs, anything can go wrong and usually does.)
Feasibility:	Practical considerations should relate to such factors as schedules, budget, personnel, and data availability.
Replicability:	If the procedures aren't reliable, they aren't trustworthy. Consistent results are at least credible. *Evaluations are only as good as their data!*
Objectivity:	Bias must be controlled for in collection, interpretation, and reporting of results.
Representativeness:	Are the data and respondents representative of the classrooms or the whole school/system where the service-learning projects were implemented? Representativeness applies to all data sources, especially community members.
Timeliness:	Data must be collected and reported in a timely fashion so that decision makers can make informed evaluations. If an evaluation is to have utility, practical and scheduled reports must be made available to relevant audiences.
Pervasiveness:	Do the audiences and decision makers get the data when they need them, and do all relevant audiences get the required data?

Protocol:	Evaluations need to be conducted in a legal manner with regard to the rights of data sources and audiences. Professional courtesy can be very helpful in implementing an evaluation, and failure in this area can sabotage the entire effort. Questions of confidentiality are of paramount importance.
Ethics:	There are a whole lot of considerations related to rights of privacy, full and frank public disclosure, confidentiality, and the use of human subjects. Legal requirements and fiscal responsibility are also critical.

A more comprehensive set of standards (with case studies) can be found in the *Standards for Evaluations of Educational Programs, Projects, and Materials* (Joint Committee, 1994). A synopsis of the Standards is presented in appendix B.

A Note about Ethics

In addition to commonsense guidelines, such as respect for the privacy of participants and minimizing the intrusion of the evaluation into the lives of the participants and the ongoing school program, evaluators need to keep in mind scientific and interpersonal parameters of ethical behaviors. The following principles have been adopted by the American Evaluation Association. An ethical evaluator needs to:

- conduct systematic data-based inquiries;
- provide competent performance to stakeholders;
- ensure that evaluations are conducted honestly and with integrity;
- respect the security, dignity, and self-worth of evaluation respondents, program participants, clients, and other stakeholders; and
- strive to articulate and take into account the diversity of interests and values in general and public welfare.

Evaluation may be formal or informal, but it should be done because a better experience or product will result.

Referenceography

Caracelli, V. J., & Greene, J. C. (1993). Data analysis strategies for mixed-method evaluation designs. *Educational Evaluation and Policy Analysis* 15(2), 195–207.

Greene, J. C., Caracelli, V. J., & Graham, W. F. (1989). Toward a conceptual framework for mixed-method evaluation designs. *Educational Evaluation and Policy Analysis*, 11(3), 255–274.

Hedin, D., & Conrad, D. (1990). Learning from experience: Experience is the best teacher or is it? In *Combining service and learning: A resource book for community service*. Raleigh, NC: NSIEE.

Joint Committee on Standards for Educational Evaluation (1994). *Standards for evaluations of educational programs, projects, and materials*. New York: McGraw-Hill.

Neal, M., Shumer, R., & Gorak, K. S. (1994). *Evaluation: The key to improving service-learning programs*. Minneapolis: Center for Experiential and Service-Learning, University of Minnesota.

Patton, M. Q. (1987). *How to use qualitative methods in evaluation*. Newbury Park, CA: Sage.

Payne, D. A. (1974). *Curriculum evaluation (Commentaries on purpose, process, product)*. Lexington, MA: D. C. Heath.

Payne, D. A. (1994). *Designing educational project and program evaluations*. Boston: Kluwer.

Rossi, P. H., & Freeman, H. E. (1993). *Evaluation—A systematic approach* (Fifth Edition). Newbury Park, CA: Sage.

Sanders, J. R. (1992). *Evaluating school programs: An educators guide*. Newbury Park, CA: Corwin.

Scriven, M. (1991). *Evaluation thesaurus*. Newbury Park, CA: Sage.

Stake, R. E. (Ed.). (1975). *Evaluating the arts in education: A responsive approach*. Columbus, OH: Merrill.

Stake, R. E. (1983). Program evaluation, particularly responsive evaluation. In G. F. Madaus, M. S. Scriven, & D. L. Stufflebeam (Eds.) *Evaluation models* (Viewpoints on educational and human service evaluation) (pp. 287–310). Boston: Kluwer-Nijhoff.

Worthen, B. R., Sanders, J. R., & Fitzpatrick, J. L. (1997). *Educational evaluation: Alternative approaches and practical guidelines* (Second Edition). New York: Longman.

Case Study

The case study presented in the following chapters (3–8) is true, only the names have been changed to protect the innocent. The effort described was the successful result of an application to the state Department of Education to request funds for a service-learning project. The applications were competitive and were rated by a panel of experts from around the state.

The service-learning project took place in a small rural primary school (PK–2). The entire school (Nurture Primary School) was involved, including custodians, lunchroom staff, and bus drivers. The school contained 30 classes, 75 staff members, and 553 students. The students were distributed as follows: PreK, 95; K, 145; first, 155; and second, 158. Of these 553 students, 63 percent qualified for free or reduced breakfast and lunch. Single-parent homes comprise 27 percent of all family settings.

The community is a small one, particularly when compared with surrounding counties. Very few businesses or industries of any size are present, although pulpwood processing is very active. The exception is a very large kaolin (clay/chalk) mining and transportation operation, a very significant employer in the area, and the economy could be devastated by any cutback in production. The small size of the community limits the resources available for the vocational exploration or social growth of many students.

A needs assessment was conducted by the students. Major public and private organizations were identified by teachers, students, and the local Chamber of Commerce for students to contact and survey. The basic question asked was, "Do you see any projects associated with your organization where our school could make a contribution?" The act of conducting the needs assessment itself energized relations between the community and school. It was a tremendous opportunity for the community to see the school's outreach. Parents in particular were excited about the possibility of a school-wide project.

Aggregation of the needs assessment data revealed that the top projects in terms of frequency of mention were:

- Wildflower plantings on highways in and out of town
- Offer of services to county homeless shelter
- Intergenerational project with local nursing home
- Landscaping around courthouse
- Assistance with care at local animal shelter

Three

Asking the Right Questions

Although it's an overused metaphor, goals and objectives really are like signposts on the road to evaluation truths. Like the dots, Xs, and icons on a map, goals, and objectives are elements in planning and implementing an evaluation design. If you don't ask questions, you won't get answers. If you ask the wrong questions, you get bad information.

Goals and Objectives

The focus of this chapter is on objectives, particularly evaluation objectives. That fact should not overshadow the important role that goals must play in evaluating service-learning. What we are talking about is two levels of specificity. A goal will present either a content or activity intent for the classroom or community. The goals selected will be derived from the needs assessment conducted, one hopes, by a committee of students, teachers, community members, and/or other interested stakeholders (anyone who has a vested interest in the specific service-learning project, active or passive). A goal is simply a broad statement of intent or purpose; from it might flow many different objectives. An example from the National Association of Partners in Education (1994) is illustrative.

> *Goal:* To engage students in the application of investigative and analytic skills through involvement in service projects.

> *Objective:* Will students in grade six improve math scores by 0.3 grade levels as measured by the Iowa Tests of Basic Skills after calculating the results of the recycling program for one school year?

The three major elements of a good objective are illustrated in the above sample evaluation objective. The objective specifies a target or audience (students), content (math scores), and a criterion (gains on the ITBS). If you don't have a target, you'll hit the wrong thing or nothing. A good objective will help the service-learning coordinator, evaluator, and participants, as well. Asking students to ask questions about what and why they are doing certain things can be revealing.

Identifying and Involving Stakeholders

Before getting into the nuts and bolts of formatting the questions and evaluating any service-learning activity, a variety of people should be consulted and involved. The degree of involvement will vary, as will the degree of interest, but there is an obligation to consult with as many as possible to generate as meaningful information as possible and help insure that the results will be used. Consultation leads to cooperation and cooperation begets (a) an effective evaluation, and (b) effective use of the results.

One needs to ask the "right" questions. The right questions most likely will lead to collection of the most relevant information, which in turn will increase the likelihood that these results will be used. Nothing is more frustrating and cost-ineffective than not using results. Unfortunately, conducting evaluations for the sake of appearance occurs all too often. These "symbolic" evaluations are often done when the results are to be used in explaining ideas, theories, or concepts, or in specific decision-making situations.

The term **stakeholder** as used here refers to individuals who have a vested interest in the outcomes of the evaluation. The word **vested** means a special concern or right. Stated another way, the results of the evaluation will have consequences for the stakeholder. The consequences could be financial, emotional, political, or professional/vocational. Following is a sampling of potential stakeholders:

- **Students:** They are both implementers and consumers of the service-learning experience, which can profoundly change their lives. They obviously have a vested interest in the activities and should have significant input into which ones are chosen and how they are implemented. A service-learning senior at Clemson University remarked at a colloquium that service-learning is **FUN** because the experience stays with you **Forever**; it helps you **Understand** yourself, your community and learning; and each time it's a **New** experience.

- **Teachers:** As with most things in the school, the burden of implementing a service-learning program rests on the teachers. They must refine their instructional approach and see that it is integrated into the curriculum. They represent a chorus of voices to be heard.

- **Parents:** An effective school program involves parents as much as possible. Service-learning programs are tailor-made for parent participation either jointly with their offspring or as volunteers.

- **Administrators:** Behind every good school and system are administrators who care and are involved. The success of service-learning programs will further enhance the educational missions of our schools and is one possible route to school reform.

- **Policy Makers and Decision Makers:** School board members and other central office personnel are stakeholders in the strongest sense of the term because they will be responsible either directly or indirectly for deciding whether a program is to be instituted, continued, discontinued, expanded, or curtailed.

- **Program Sponsors:** Organizations that initiate and fund programs are obviously stakeholders. A positive evaluation can help "spread the word."

- **Programs/School Partners:** Those public and private organizations, especially businesses and industry, that are direct contributors to the ongoing service collaborators will want to help contribute goals and evaluation data. Because of the importance of preparing our youth for the world of work, business and industry partners might be nurtured and identified as a special targeted group.

- **Community Members:** The local community and government will want to know how service-learning has transformed the school and brought it closer.

What kinds of questions might these groups want answered?

Kinds of Evaluation Questions

The kinds of evaluation questions to be addressed will be dictated by the information requirements of decision makers, and the nature and state of service-learning innovations that are proposed or have been implemented. Some questions might be considered **formative**—for example: How can we improve the materials used in the elementary mathematics curriculum to incorporate a service component? Or questions might be **summative** in nature—for example: Is the current approach to the teaching of writing the best way to sample student performance? The most important of questions might be referred to as **generative**, such as: Why are we doing this particular kind of project? What do we hope to achieve? What will we learn from the experience? and What effect will the project have on others? In any event, the evaluation question should be based on objectives or goals. We need goals and objectives to help us frame the right evaluation questions.

Following is a list of sample evaluation questions that might be asked about service-learning. Additions to the list and the kinds of questions are limited only by the creativity of the evaluator.

Focus Category	*Sample Evaluation Questions*
1. General Needs Assessment	What community service needs could students address?
2. Individual Needs Assessment	How do our students feel about the concept of civic responsibility? What do students know about the ecology of our area?
3. Curriculum Design	How have service-learning activities been integrated into the science curriculum?
4. Classroom Process	Are teachers following the service-learning procedures as suggested in the fall staff development meetings?
5. Materials of Instruction	Have the science lab materials been modified so they are aligned with service-learning objectives?
6. Teacher Effectiveness	To what extent has teacher use of service-learning activities reduced discipline problems?
7. Learner Motivation	Has attendance improved for those students participating in service-learning activities who were previously identified as recalcitrant?
8. Learning Environment	Have student attitudes toward school improved?
9. Staff Development	What were teacher reactions to last week's workshop on writing service-learning lesson plans?
10. Community Involvement	How does the Chamber of Commerce feel about the park beautification project recently completed by local college students?
11. School Outcomes	Have the science subtest scores on the high school graduation test been influenced positively by the introduction of school-wide ecology service-learning activities?
12. Resource Allotment	Have school budgets reflected the increase in service-learning activities throughout the system? Have external funds been sought in support of service-learning projects?
13. Instructional Methods	How have classroom instruction, particularly methods, been changed by the introduction of service-learning activities?
14. Decision Making	What impact will the change to block scheduling have on the nature and extent of service-learning programs in the school?

Now that we have identified the information needs of audiences, how do we go about asking the questions?

Formatting Questions

How an evaluation question is phrased depends on a number of factors. Among these are (a) who wants the information, (b) when they want the information, (c) how easy it will be to get the information, (d) how long does service activity last, (e) what research says about the activity, and, most important, (f) what decisions and actions will be taken as a result of collecting, summarizing, and reporting the results of answering the question. In general, the more focused the question, the more meaningful the answer.

Seven different, but related question forms can be used.

> **Open-Ended:** What will be (has been) the effect of service-learning activities on students?

Such phraseology, while providing a general framework for collecting and examining data, still has sufficient latitude to allow the evaluator to go in a number of different directions relative to what evidence will be used to finally evaluate the question. With a question this broad, one could go the academic or service route. Asking the question this way probably would be done only when one has no or very little idea what to expect, but this would be the exception rather than the rule.

> **Focused:** What will be the effect of service-learning activities on student self-concept?

With this format we focus on the type of change we hope to observe. Using an old-fashioned term, what is the **dependent** measure? Our expectations might spring from past research or experience. We immediately see the need to look for a measure of self-concept or perhaps we might have to create one.

> **Status:** Will students participating in service-learning activities evidence a positive self-concept? (A level, indexed perhaps by a percent or percentile rank score, might be specified.)
>
> or
>
> Is there a positive relationship between self-concept and participation in service-learning activities?

This is a "correlation" question where data on student self-concept are statistically correlated with some quantitative index of student participation. Directionality has been introduced, however.

> **Comparative Relative Internal:** Will students who participate in service-learning activities show an increase in self-concept?
>
> or
>
> **Comparative Relative External:** Will students who participate in service-learning activities evidence more positive self-concept increases than those students not participating?

The "standard" here is a **relative** one. In the first case, the standard is internal being derived from a comparison of pre and post (before and after) scores for the **same** group. In the second case, a comparison is made between those experiencing service-learning and another comparable group not having that experience. An **absolute** standard might also be specified.

> **Comparative Absolute Internal:** Will students participating in service-learning activities show at least 35 percent better attitude toward science scores?
>
> or
>
> **Comparative Absolute External:** Will students participating in service-learning activities evidence 20 percent better attitude toward science survey scores than nonparticipating students?

The absolute standard can be negotiated among the faculty, evaluator, and administrators, or some systematic standard setting procedure might be used (Popham, 1990, pp. 343–368).

When doing evaluations you are always faced with resource-allocation conflicts. Best professional judgment should lead you to select and focus on those goals and objectives that are likely to bring about the greatest positive change and that are judged to be most important by the majority of stakeholders. One might even get the stakeholders to rank order the goals and/or objectives in terms of their perceived value and select them in consultation with students.

The best professional judgment will need to be applied in deciding which evaluation question(s) to target. A frequently followed realistic road is that of compromise, as long as professional integrity is not subverted. Even with a very large budget, employment of every known relative, and all the cooperation in the world, it is impossible to investigate or respond to all potentially relevant evaluation questions. It would seem reasonable to focus on a limited number of questions and do the best possible job on those.

Referenceography

Berk, R. A. (1986). A consumer's guide to setting performance standards on criterion-referenced tests. *Review of Educational Research*, 56(1), 132–172.

Bryk, A. S. (1983). *Stakeholder-based evaluation* (New Direction for Program Evaluation, No. 17). San Francisco: Jossey-Bass.

Morris, L. L., & Taylor Fitz-Gibbon, C. (1978). *How to deal with goals and objectives*. Beverly Hills, CA: Sage.

National Association of Partners in Education, Inc. (1994). *Service-learning & business/education partnerships-A guide for service-learning coordinators* (Second Revision, 1996). Alexandria, VA: National Association of Partners in Education.

Popham, W. J. (1990). *Modern educational measurement* (Second Edition). Englewood Cliffs, NJ: Prentice Hall.

Case Study

After much deliberation, it was decided to develop an intergenerational project labeled Adopt-a-Senior. A local nursing home (Pine Tree Manor) was enthusiastic about joining with the school in a service-learning effort. From the Manor's standpoint there was a great need because 85 percent of the sixty residents had no regular visitors. One of the major factors in deciding on the nursing home was its proximity to the school. In addition, interaction with seniors is in a sense preparation for the future. A program was designed to help students to develop greater courtesy, cooperation, mutual respect, and interdependence with others resulting in an effort to create a better society.

Three broad project goals served as a framework for the project:

- to facilitate learning between old and young,
- to use the individual and group talents that will help bridge the gap between the generations, and
- to enhance courtesy, cooperation, and respect among the residents and students.

In a real sense this could be characterized as a character education project that incidentally follows a state mandate to address this topic formally throughout the curriculum.

Staff Development

Upon receiving a $5,500 grant (excluding evaluation costs), a staff development program was initiated that included the following topics discussed on alternating Tuesday afternoons:

- Orientation to capabilities and limitations of Pine Tree Manor residents by Director
- Slides and videos of residents in their environment
- First Aid and CPR
- Session with residents by primary school teacher to orient them to working with young students
- Presentation on death and dying by hospice

Implementation

Each grade alternately took responsibility for a month's activities. The only common activity was that each month students were responsible for creating and delivering birthday cards, cake, and singing "Happy Birthday" for that month's resident celebrants. Visits ranged in length from thirty minutes to one hour. Anything longer pushed the attention limits of the primary students.

Following are sample objectives, activities, and academic referents by grade:

Grade	Objective	Activity	Academic Link
Pre-Kindergarten	Students will create Christmas decorations.	Collect and make ornaments, collect and assemble fruit and candy baskets, and create Christmas cards.	Art Math Social Studies
Kindergarten	Students will become familiar with background and experiences of residents.	Create a book of of pictures and stories (biographies) about residents.	Social Studies Writing
First	Students will identify a plant and its parts, observe and record plant growth.	Read about and discuss parts of a plant Residents and students will plant a seed and care for it. Keep a daily record of growth.	Science Reading Math
Second	Students will be able to measure, follow directions, and dramatize a story.	Make applesauce and dramatize story of Johnny Appleseed for residents.	Health Math (measuring) Reading

Other activities might be Valentine and Halloween cards; providing music for a "senior prom"; publishing a health records brochure; creating "necessity" pouches; making or buying blankets or pillows; creating turkey/Thanksgiving wreaths, centerpieces, placemats; making birdfeeders; windsocks for residents; creating a fitness exercise video and giving it to center; assembling craft kits for residents; and working with a local pet store or animal shelter to supply pets for residents. Pine Tree Manor has two "house dogs" the residents love and a number of caged birds.

The culminating experience will be a Fun Day at Pine Tree Manor where all will join in a celebration of the project. Media coverage will be secured.

THOUGHT QUESTION

Considering the foregoing information about Adopt-a-Senior and the content of this chapter, think about, or better yet, write out some evaluation questions.

Realizing that evaluation questions and designs are compromises between ideal practice and realistic limits, the following evaluation questions were posed for the comprehensive school-wide project:

EQ_1: Will students who engaged in a nursing home service-learning experience change their stereotypic attitudes toward the elderly more than comparable non-service-learning students?

EQ_2: Will students who engaged in a nursing home service-learning experience enhance their attitudes toward reading more than comparable non-service-learning students?

EQ_3: Will students who engaged in a nursing home service-learning experience enhance their reading proficiency more than comparable non-service-learning students?

EQ_4: Will students who engaged in a nursing home service-learning project positively evaluate their experience and service activity?

EQ_5: Will nursing home residents favorably evaluate their intergenerational experience?

Four

Evaluating Service-Learning Knowledge and Performance Outcomes

The next three chapters address the measurement and evaluation of three major kinds of outcomes: Knowledge and Performance, Writing, and Sentiments. This chapter provides an overview of some of the concepts, methods, approaches, and resources that educators might consider when faced with documenting the "knowledge and performance" impact of a service-learning program. In addition, references are made to additional resources.

Every academically linked service-learning activity has some knowledge component. Anyone charged with the responsibility of collecting information about the impact of that academic link and the service-learning activities faces a real challenge. The information needed may range from knowledge about and ability to use water quality assessment instruments to verbal descriptions of cooperative class behavior to perceptions of the value or impact of a tutoring experience. A variety of sources will need to be tapped if a complete picture of the experience/activity is to be gained. Information gathered from a variety of sources can confirm findings. It can also suggest modifications and improvements. Sometimes paper-and-pencil methods are appropriate, at other times observers serve as the instruments.

Characteristics of High-Quality Information

Following are seven desirable characteristics to be sought in any information collected to answer questions about the impact of service-learning activities. We are considering measurements as the source of information. Reliance is on quantitative and qualitative information, depending on the questions being asked—e.g., number of test questions about pollution answered correctly vs. feelings about how the recycling program could be improved.

> **Relevance.** Relevance is the correspondence between the information and the intent or objective in gathering it. It might be the match between a test item and an instructional objective, or the match between a series of planned observations and projected teacher-student or student-student interactions. In the measurement sense, relevance is the primary contributor to validity or the degree to which measurement is a true and accurate reflection of the variable of interest.

> **Balance.** Any measurement needs a framework or plan for its development. The extent to which the developed measure corresponds to the ideal measure reflects balance. In developing an achievement test, for example, a blueprint in the form of a table of specifications is created whereby content and outcomes are summarized in a 2×2 table. Entries in the cells reflect the proportion of instructional time devoted to those objectives. The test is then built according to those proportions, resulting in a balanced measure. Any multidimensional instrument can benefit from the application of this concept. It is a particularly important concept for classroom assessment.

> **Specificity.** One assessment approach to use if one is interested in isolating the effect of a specific service-learning exercise or activity is to develop an assessment task that

would show before and after performance differences. An improvement in "scores" criterion would be used whether the task is cognitive—e.g., a knowledge objective about life-forms in a local creek, or affective—e.g., attitude toward senior citizens.

Efficiency. Basically we are looking for the greatest number of meaningful responses per unit of time. Gathering data costs time and money, so we want to conserve our resources and allocate them to the most important objectives. A balance among time available to collect the data, cost, requirements for scoring and summarization, and relevance should be sought.

Objectivity. Do experts agree on the meaning of the information? With regard to paper- and-pencil essay exams, for example, do different scorers or raters come up with the same results? If behavioral observations are involved, will different observers "see" the same thing? Along the same lines, given a series of extensive field notes from participant observers, will different ethnographers come up with the same interpretation? Objectivity, then, is a characteristic of the "scoring" or the assignment of meaning to the data, rather than a description of the data collection method. This is an extremely important criterion when scoring and analyzing writing samples with rubrics.

Reliability. Reliability is a complex characteristic but generally involves consistency of measurement. Consistency of measurement might be judged in terms of time, items, scorers, examinees, examiners, or accuracy of classifications. It also has important applications when dealing with qualitative data. These might relate to such activities as interobserver agreement and consistency in drawing inferences from observational data or written descriptions.

Fairness. The criterion of fairness relates to a wide range of characteristics, ranging from freedom from bias (gender, ethnic, or racial) to the collection of information in a manner that allows all students, for example, an equal chance to demonstrate their knowledge or skill. Everyone should play by the same rules, and the rules should be the same for everyone.

These criteria, then, represent characteristics that need to be kept in mind when developing or selecting measuring devices. The seven categories are obviously not mutually exclusive—for example, an irrelevant test question also would not be fair. The criteria represent targets for our evaluation arrows.

Evaluating Knowledge Outcomes

Effective educational assessment results from planning, imaginative and skillful question writing, careful formulation of questions into a total test, and fair, proper administration, scoring, and interpretation. A well-written question is a thing of beauty. Effectiveness also depends on the quality of instruction preceding assessment and on the intelligent subsequent interpretation and use of scores. It is assumed that all students have had an equal opportunity to learn the material on which they are tested. We should **always** go over every assessment with students. Planning, whose importance is often underestimated, involves decisions about learning outcomes, the contexts in which they are most likely to be demonstrated, and the kinds of stimuli necessary or likely to elicit them. Question or item writing follows logically from a logical test development sequence, and—make no mistake—it is a difficult and time-consuming task. We do, however, make very important decisions about curricula, students, programs, activities, experiences, and institutions on the basis of assessments that we have prepared. Therefore our maximum efforts are required.

Assessing ongoing classroom instruction that contains some new, specially designed academically linked service activities is not much different from the classroom evaluations that the teacher has traditionally implemented. Thinking of classroom learning in terms of knowledge, comprehension and application allows the teacher to use some of our old measurement friends, the objective item type.

Preliminary Considerations

Following are five principles that should be considered as you prepare to create questions.

- Make adequate provision for measuring all the important outcomes of instruction.
- The test and its questions or tasks should reflect the approximate emphases given various objectives.
- The nature of the questions must consider the nature of the group to be examined.
- The nature of the questions must account for the conditions under which the data are to be gathered.
- The nature of the questions must account for the purpose the question is to serve for decision makers.

Question Types

Table 4.1 contains an overview of the advantages and disadvantages of common question types. Choice of question type will depend on subject matter, perhaps reading level of student and amount of time available to collect information, among other things.

Some suggestions for constructing various objective item types are collected in the checklist presented in figure 4.1. Following are some sample items dealing with environmental issues.

Ecology is best described as the study of pollution and its control. (F)

Soil pollution is generally due to poisonous metals. (T)

A paper manufacturing company in your area produces large amounts of sulfuric acid as a waste by-product. In spite of efforts to dispose of the waste carefully, some acid continually escapes recovery and pollutes a nearby river, affecting wildlife and recreation. The company employs many area residents. Which of the following solutions to help stop the pollution would the community prefer?

a. moving the company to a more isolated area and giving the worker the option to move,
b. adding a substance to the escaping acid to neutralize it,
c. adding an acid with a higher Ph to the escaping acid, or
d. storing the escaping acid in large holding tanks and then taking it to an industrial waste landfill.

Table 4.1   Advantages and Disadvantages of Various Question Types

Question Type	Advantage	Disadvantage
Short Answer (Direct Question, Completion)	Natural in form Good measure of knowledge Effect of guessing minimized	Scoring not always objective Depends on ability to write Can be trivial questions
Constant Alternative (True-False)	Can administer large number per unit time Quick survey knowledge Easy to write Efficiency in administration and scoring	Guessing can influence Language critical Little diagnostic value
Changing Alternative (Multiple-choice)	Flexibility in outcomes measured Effect of guessing minimized Tends to be free of response sets Efficiency in administration and scoring	Good ones difficult to write
Matching	Quick knowledge survey Efficiency in administration and scoring	Susceptible to irrelevant cues, implausible alternatives, and awkward arrangement
Essay	Sample of student thinking Can be used to measure subject matter, communication skills, or, problem-solving skills	Reliability of scoring May have content validity problems

Figure 4.1 Checklist of Achievement Item Writing Principles

Item Content	Yes	No
1. Does item deal with content of sufficient importance and significance?	___	___
2. Are various cognitive outcomes measured?	___	___
3. Is content too specific?	___	___
4. Is item content up-to-date?		
5. Is content unambiguous so that student does not have to make unwarranted interpretations?	___	___
6. Are items grouped by content?	___	___
7. Is content appropriate for grade and ability level?	___	___
8. Are vocabulary and readability levels appropriate for examinees?	___	___

Item Structure		
9. Is problem statement clearly expressed?	___	___
10. Is test free from interrelated items (items give answer to other items)?	___	___
11. Is best question format used for given objective?	___	___
12. Is item free from ambiguous wording?	___	___
13. Is item free from irrelevant cues?	___	___
14. Can answers to questions be scored objectively?	___	___
15. Are multiple-choice answers mutually exclusive?	___	___
16. Are multiple-choice answers plausible?	___	___
17. Are multiple-choice answers grammatically parallel?	___	___
18. Are multiple-choice answers of comparable length?	___	___
19. Is test free from trick or catch questions?	___	___

Alice grows violets. She has six red and six white violets. She heard that violets produce more flowers when they receive morning sunlight. She made this hypothesis:

"When violets receive morning sunlight rather than afternoon sunlight, they will produce more flowers."

Which plan should she choose to test this?
a. Set all her violets in the morning sun. Count the number of flowers.
b. Set three white violets in the morning sun. Set the other three white violets in the afternoon sun. Do not study the red ones at all.
c. Set all of her plants in the morning sun for four months. Count the number of flowers produced during this time. Then set all of the plants in the afternoon sun for four months. Count the number of flowers produced during this time.
d. Set three red and three white violets in the morning sun. Place the other three red and three white violets in the afternoon sun. Count the number of flowers produced by each plant for four months.

The burning of fossil fuels increases the carbon dioxide content of the atmosphere. What is the most immediate effect of this increasing amount of carbon dioxide likely to have on our planet?

a. A warmer climate
b. A cooler climate
c. Decreased relative humidity
d. Increased relative humidity

Classroom assessments are not the only source of relevant evaluation information.

Selecting Standardized Achievement Tests

Although classroom assessments are the best single source of information about the academic link in service-learning, under the right controlled conditions, standardized achievement tests can yield valuable data. The selection or use of such measures is both an art and a science. The major advantage of standardized measures is just that, they are standardized with regard to administration and, to some extent, interpretation. Make no mistake, however, that in our test-crazed society, there is a real danger of overinterpretation. Harried and harassed educators are always on the lookout for quick and cost-efficient answers. Standardized achievement tests also offer comprehensive coverage of content. This can be a blessing and a curse. It is a blessing in that a national sampling of curricula and textbooks has been tapped for common learning outcomes. Because they are standardized they are also reliable. It is a curse in that there may not be a good fit between the test and the local instructional programs and objectives. Bias results, and misinformation follows. Another danger is that the comprehensive content coverage of the test or battery does not allow for collection of more narrowly focused relevant information. And make no mistake, it takes a Herculean effort to move those averages on standardized achievement tests.

But let's assume for the moment that we have the opportunity to select an achievement test or that one has been thrust upon us. We have an obligation to learn as much as possible about the test's developmental and technical characteristics to make the most intelligent use of the scores, although standard scores, percentile ranks, and normal curve equivalents can be scary.

Locating Information about Tests

It would be impossible to list, let alone critically evaluate, all those tests that might interest a particular instructor, administrator, or evaluator. A potential user needs answers to such questions as: (a) What types of tests are available that will yield the kinds of information I am interested in? (b) What do the "experts" say about the tests I am interested in? (c) What research has been undertaken on this test? (d) What statistical data relating to validity and reliability are available for examination? (e) With what groups can I legitimately use this test? Answers to these and many other relevant questions can be found in one or more of the following resources:

1. *Mental Measurements Yearbooks*
2. Test reviews in professional journals
3. Test manuals and specimen sets
4. Text and reference books on testing
5. Bibliographies of tests and testing literature
6. Educational and psychological abstract indexes
7. Publisher's test catalogs
8. Test critiques (for example, Keyser & Sweetland, 1988)

Any competent librarian can help you access other sources of information, such as *Tests in Print, Directory of Selected National Testing Programs*, Educational Testing Service Test Collection catalogs, *Index to Tests Used in Educational Dissertations, Educational Index, Dissertation Abstracts International, Psychological Abstracts*, and the Educational Resources Information Center (especially the one in Tests and Measurements), which publishes *Resources in Education and Current Index to Journals in Education*. Computer searches of these and other databases—e.g. through (DIALOG) can greatly facilitate information gathering.

Of the resources listed, the first three are probably the most immediately informative. These three sources are discussed in turn, with the types of information that each provides.

The Mental Measurements Yearbooks

Probably the most useful sources of evaluative information about all types of commercial tests are the *Mental Measurements Yearbooks (MMY)*. Originated by the late Dr. Oscar K. Buros, they are now the province of the Buros Institute of Mental Measurements at the University of Nebraska. Up-to-date and comprehensive bibliographies, test reviews, and book reviews are published in the *Yearbooks*, thirteen of which have been published to date. *The Thirteenth Mental Measurements Yearbook* (Impara & Plake, 1998) contains descriptive information on 369 tests and 693 test reviews by 408 different authors and includes 4,362 references. Buros's goal was to develop in the potential user and publisher a critical attitude toward tests and testing, to facilitate communication, and to significantly increase the quality of published tests. Specifically, Buros wanted the *Yearbooks* (a) to provide information about tests published as separates throughout the English-speaking world; (b) to present frankly critical test reviews written by testing and subject specialists representing various viewpoints; (c) to provide extensive bibliographies of verified references on the construction, use, and validity of specific tests; (d) to make readily available the critical portions of test reviews appearing in professional journals; and (e) to present fairly exhaustive listings of new and revised books on testing, along with evaluative excerpts from representative reviews which these books receive in professional journals. The *Yearbooks* have made a significant and lasting contribution toward these ends.

There is also an easily computer-searchable database for the *MMY*. Based on the *MMY* classification schemes, users can access the *MMY* database with a variety of algorithms to isolate tests for specific variables, populations, price, publication date, and so forth. Between *Yearbooks*, the Buros Institute publishes a softback *MMY Supplement* with the most recent test reviews.

Test Reviews in Professional Journals

Despite the availability of such authoritative comprehensive sources as the *Yearbooks*, it is often difficult to locate immediately current data on new or old tests. Research data or questions related to reliability, validity, and usability, and occasional test reviews are periodically carried in the following journals: *Journal of Educational Measurement, Applied Measurement in Education, Measurement and Evaluation in Guidance, Applied Psychological Measurement*, and *Journal of Psychological Assessment*. An excellent source of validity studies is the publication, *Educational and Psychological Measurement*.

Test Manuals and Specimen Sets

After preliminary decisions have narrowed the field, a potential user should probably obtain specimen sets from publishers. Such a set usually contains a copy of the test questions, scoring key, answer sheets, examiner's manual, and occasionally a technical manual. The sets, available at a nominal cost, should be ordered on official school or institution letterhead because most publishers attempt to ensure that their materials are distributed to qualified individuals only. If there is any question about the qualifications required to purchase a particular test, consult the publisher's catalog.

Once a user has been granted access to a particular test, additional guidelines relating to test security must be followed. These guidelines include the following:

1. Test taker must not receive test answers before beginning the test.
2. Test questions are not to be reproduced or paraphrased in any way by a school, college, or any organization or person.
3. Access to test materials is limited to persons with a responsible, professional interest who will safeguard their use.
4. Test materials and scores are to be released only to persons qualified to interpret and use them properly.
5. If a test taker or the parent of a child who has taken the test wishes to examine responses or results, the parent or test taker is permitted to read a copy of the test and the test answers of the test taker in the presence of a representative of the school, college, or institution that administered the test.

The test manual is the most informative and readily accessible source of information about a specific test. Directions for administering and scoring the test, brief statistical information about validity, reliability, and norms, a description of the test's development, and suggestions for interpreting and using the test results constitute the usual content of the manual. The reviewer should remember, however, that the publisher has a vested interest, and all tests should be evaluated critically.

Selecting an Achievement Test

After informally reviewing several tests in a particular area and making a preliminary decision about the purpose of testing and the projected uses of the test data, the instructor would profit from a detailed examination of two or three tests. A set of evaluative questions that have been found useful in judging a test for possible use in schools is reprinted below. The first eight categories are essentially descriptive, but nevertheless important. For example, such factors as the affiliation of the author and the copyright data illuminate such significant criteria as credibility, authenticity, and recency.

In undertaking a "critical analysis," you will consult many sources. (Refer to earlier pages for information on identifying references.) In addition, it would be worthwhile for the test evaluator to refer to *Standards for Educational and Psychological Testing* (American Psychological Association, 1999) for assistance in identifying criteria for many of the variables described in this outline. It is usually a good idea to record the comments, evaluations, and sources consulted during the review process.

Outline for Critical Analysis of a Standardized Achievement Test

1. **Title:** Note complete and exact title of test.

2. **Author:** A brief summary of professional affiliations and credentials is informative.

3. **Publisher:** Some publishers are more reputable than others. Check with experts in testing.

4. **Copyright Date:** Note dates of first publication and each revision.

5. **Level or Group for Whom Test Is Intended:** Such factors as age, grade, and ability level should be considered. What background does the author presuppose for examinees? Is the test available at different levels? If so, which ones?

6. **Forms of the Test:** What forms of the test are available? If the forms are not essentially the same, major differences should be mentioned and evaluated. What evidence is presented on equivalence of forms?

7. **Purpose and Recommended Use:** Summarize the use of the test recommended by the author.

8. **Dimensions of Areas that the Test Purports to Measure:** Give a brief definition or description of the variables involved. If the test has numerous scales (or scores), it may be necessary simply to mention the subscores and highlight only the group or distinctive scores. If at this point there is no match with local objectives or intents, you should probably terminate the review of this particular instrument.

9. **Administration:** Describe briefly. The median time required to complete the test should be indicated. If parts of the test are timed separately, note how many starting points are necessary. Are the directions easy for the test administrator to follow and the test takers to comprehend? Is special training required for valid administration? Is the test largely self-administering? Does it have any objectionable features?

10. **Scoring:** Scoring procedures should be described very briefly. Is the test planned and organized so that machine-scored answer sheets can or must be used? Is a correction for guessing justified or applied?

11. **Source of Items:** Where did the author(s) get the items? What criteria were used in item selection? Are some items taken from other tests? If so, which ones?

12. **Description of Items (Format and Content):** Briefly describe the major types of items used. Attention should be given to *item form* (for example, multiple-choice, analogy, forced-choice) and *item content* (for example, future-free symbols, nonsense syllables, food preferences, occupational titles). How many response categories are there? Note a typical example of the major type(s) of items used. It is imperative that the actual items be evaluated in light of questions a teacher would ask of the data.

13. **Statistical Item Analysis:** Was an item analysis made to determine item discrimination and difficulty? What were the results? What criteria were used to select items for the final form(s) of the instrument? What analytic techniques were used? Were checks made for gender, racial, and ethnic bias?

14. **Method and Results of Validation Reported by Publisher and Author:** For most tests this topic is related to categories 11, 12, and 13. You must ask, What was done to make the test valid and useful? Some tests are validated by expert judgment, some by an external criterion, and so on. What has the author done to demonstrate the validity of the test? What correlations with other tests are presented? Has an external criterion been used to evaluate the usefulness of the scores? This section should deal with data other than those obtained in the construction of the test. What specific "predictions" could you make from an individual's test score on the basis of the validity data presented?

15. **Validity as Determined by Others:** This is in many respects the crucial evaluative criterion. The recent literature should be consulted, and studies briefly summarized.

16. **Reliability:** State briefly how reliability was determined. Report interesting or unusual data on reliability. Was reliability computed separately for each subgroup or part of the test?

17. **Norm Group(s):** How many were involved? How were they selected? Are separate norms available for each group with whom you want to compare an individual's score-that is, norms for each sex, age level, curriculum major, occupation?

18. **Interpretation of Scores:** How are scores expressed? (Percentile ranks, standard scores, grade equivalent scores?) What is considered a "high" score? A "low" score? How are these scores interpreted?

19. **Major Evaluations by Experts:** What assumptions are examined and what questions are raised in the *Mental Measurements Yearbooks*? What do measurement experts and the journals say about the test?

20. **Cost Factors:** The initial cost of booklets and answer sheets should be considered, as well as such factors as cost of scoring, reusability of booklets, and availability of summary and research services.

21. **Distinguishing Characteristics:** What are the outstanding features of this test, its construction, and its use? Note both desirable and undesirable features.

22. **Overall Evaluation:** How well do such factors as validity, reliability, standardization, and item content coincide with the intended use of the test?

How should the information in these twenty-two categories be weighted? No universal answer can be given because the selection of a particular test or battery depends on the individual needs of specific instructors or schools. The **purpose** of testing must be foremost in the mind of the test evaluator. Such questions as What specific information is needed? and How will the test data be interpreted and used? are highly significant. Questions relating to validity, reliability, and the representativeness of the normative data should be critically reviewed and heavily weighted in the final decisions if the test is to be used in a norm-referenced way.

The critical evaluation of any standardized achievement test is a time-consuming and involved process. But considering the kinds of decisions that will be made about students and programs as a result of such tests, the expenditure of effort is more than justified.

Standardized tests, particularly achievement tests, represent valuable tools to be used to help realize human potential. They are sources of information, but they are not the *only* source of information. Legal and professional efforts are being made to ensure fair and equitable use of tests, but we should ascribe any shortcomings of use to the user rather than to the tool. Education and training are the major avenue to more informed test use and decision making.

Let us not forget the admonition of Walter S. Monroe, who wrote in his 1924 text, *Educational Tests and Measurements*, "Standardized tests and scales are not 'playthings.'"

Knowledge is a great thing, whether collected through classroom assessment or standardized measure, but for it to be productive one has to be able to do something with it, to turn it into an application, solve a problem, or use it in a performance.

Evaluating Applied Performance

Over the last several years, we have seen movement in classrooms toward a somewhat nontraditional philosophy about educational assessment. Although the basic elements are not new, they are being organized in a new way that—it is hoped—will provide stronger links among instruction, learning, and measurement. This approach has been variously termed authentic assessment, direct assessment, alternative assessment, or **performance assessment**. The umbrella term performance assessment will be used in the remainder of this chapter. What is desired is a more operational definition of what students can do, what skills they possess, and what problems they can solve. Definite emphasis is placed on higher-order thinking skills. This philosophy developed in partial response to dissatisfaction expressed about some current testing practices, especially multiple-choice tests. Particular dissatisfaction has been expressed concerning state-mandated testing programs established for accountability with their predominant emphasis on minimum competencies and basic skills, and norm-referenced interpretations. There is a desire to reduce the "inference gap" between assessment and criterion, which, it is hoped, will yield greater validity.

The notion and practice of performance assessment is not new; we have been doing it for many years. Assessments of writing skills, typing, computer applications, science laboratory skills, foreign language learning, and a variety of physical education, art, and music outcomes all qualify as performance assessments. Educators appear to want more hands-on assessment where actual student behaviors as well as products can be examined.

Among the more important general characteristics of modern performance assessment are the following:

1. **Value beyond the assessment itself.** The assessment task should be meaningful in and of itself and not derive value just from being a "test."

2. **Student-constructed response.** Having a record of an actual student behavior observed and evaluated or an evaluated product brings criterion and assessment closer together.

3. **Realistic focus.** This characteristic relates to the contemporary need to show students that they are involved in "meaningful" (real-world) learning that will have an ultimate tangible payoff.

4. **Application of knowledge.** The need to measure problem-solving and critical thinking skills results in these educational outcomes being reemphasized.

5. **Multiple data sources.** A variety of approaches will enhance validity and reliability and allow greater adaptability to individual student differences. This characteristic obviously represents a desire to address the increasing diversity in our classrooms.

6. **Objectives-based and criterion-referenced.** Having objectives to guide development and interpretation contributes to the relevance of the assessment and its validity. Having this characteristic allows the assessment to meet both summative and formative goals.

7. **Reliability.** Consistency is a prerequisite in any assessment from administration to performance and scoring.

8. **Multiple approaches.** The student, with advance notice, should have some latitude in determining how the assessment will be documented.

9. **Multidimensional in structure.** This characteristic addresses the comprehensive integration and combination of skills and knowledge.

10. **Multidimensional scores.** A single summative score is less meaningful and has less diagnostic value than several subscores.

One example of trying to do things differently with modern authentic assessment is **portfolio assessment**. Portfolios are used at all levels of education. A portfolio is a collection of student products intentionally selected to represent a variety of achievements over a specified period of time, usually a school year. The portfolio must include the actual student products, a statement of why each was included, and the criteria used in evaluating them. A final item sometimes included is a student self-evaluation of selected products or the portfolio as a whole. Student progress can therefore be documented and evaluated over time. The opportunity for student creativity—for example, in writing—is significant. In addition, this approach creates a real sense of ownership and investment in assessment. Of course, good teachers have been doing this kind of thing for a long time. Assessment definitely is integrated into learning when approached in this manner. The aggregation of portfolio data useful in evaluation at other than the student level is difficult if not impossible because of the idiosyncratic nature of the portfolios. Creative methods for identifying and synthesizing themes and trends across portfolios are needed.

Despite performance assessment's obvious advantages, its disadvantages are evident. The first relates to time. Developing and evaluating a representative performance assessment, particularly a portfolio, is labor-intensive. And from a physical standpoint, only a limited number of objectives can be documented in any depth. If we are focusing on numerous respondents, time and cost can be significant factors indeed.

If modern assessments truly represent operational definitions of what we want our students to accomplish, then "teaching to the test" might not be considered an academic crime. Table 4.2 compares current performance assessment trends with traditional trends.

Developing Performance Assessments

Much instructional time, particularly in the early grades, is devoted to developing specific performance skills. Examples are laboratory work, handwriting, physical skills, speaking, social skills, music, artistic and dramatic skills, essay writing, and a variety of vocational skills. We are interested in the products of learning, of course, but we are also concerned with *how* the student arrives at his or her product. Often the technique or skill development can be considered an end in itself or so intimately tied to the product as to be inseparable. An overview of the characteristic of performance assessment is presented in table 4.3.

Table 4.2   Comparison of Characteristics of Performance Assessment and Traditional Educational Measurement

Characteristic	Performance Assessment	Traditional Management
Intent	Emphasis on improvement	Focus on accountability
Nature of Objectives	Integrated sets of objectives Higher-order outcomes	Tends to isolate lower-level and separate objectives
Nature of Task(s)	Variety of methods, especially open-ended	Tends to be structured
Administration	Can be time-consuming	Efficient
Nature of Response	Usually student-constructed response, supply Oral, process, written, product, observation of performance	Fixed-response, selection
Scoring and Reporting	Can be complex, multidimensional	Objective, efficient, machine scorable Single global score
Reliability	Can reach acceptable levels with training	Almost always high
Cost	Can be very high	Per unit cost is modest
Impact on Student	Less threatening	Can be anxiety-provoking, especially high-stakes tests

The key to developing a performance assessment is stimulation; most paper-and-pencil devices suffer from artificiality. Developmental situations in which an individual can exhibit real-life behaviors generally increase the relevance and accuracy of the assessment.

Table 4.3 Performance Assessment Characteristics

Characteristic	Example	Characteristic	Example
Purpose	Assess ability to translate knowledge and under- into action	Potential Sources of Inaccurate Assessment	Poor exercises Too few samples of performance Vague criteria Poor rating procedures Poor test conditions
Typical Exercise	Written prompt or natural event framing the kind of performance required	Influence on Learning	Emphasizes use of available skill and knowledge in relevant problem contexts
Student's Response	Plan, construct, and deliver original response	Keys to Success	Carefully prepared performance exercises Clear performance expectations Careful, thoughtful rating Time to rate performance
Scoring	Check attributes present, rate proficiency demonstrated, or describe performance via anecdote	Major Disability	Difficult and time-consuming to develop and score Cost
Major Advantages	Provide rich evidence of performance skills Meaningful results		
Sources of Error	Poorly written tasks Too few tasks Unreliable scoring Limited content sample		

After Stiggins, 1987.

Performance assessment's advantage is that it can be both a teaching and testing method. When presented in a game-like format, particularly to young children, simulations also are fun. Performance assessments such as simulations allow data to be collected for events or situations that occur only rarely. Think, for example, of flight simulation used to train jet pilots. Simulation of an emergency, such as the loss of an engine, can be used to train the test pilot's skills. The dynamic functions of the human body and interactions with disease processes can be simulated to train and test doctors. Role playing is an effective and inexpensive method you can use to examine interpersonal communication and counseling skills. Building a "city" in an elementary classroom (with post office, supermarket, bank, and so on) is another practical kind of simulation.

In educational settings, we must consider practical limitations, so developing a simulation test involves compromises. In making these compromises we must

1. determine through careful analysis the critical aspects of the criterion situation to be assessed;
2. determine the minimum accuracy or fidelity needed for each aspect and estimate the worth of increasing fidelity beyond the minimum;
3. develop a scheme for representing a reasonably comprehensive set of tasks within the limits of available resources; and
4. adjust comprehensiveness and fidelity, compromising as necessary to balance considerations but paying primary attention to the aspects shown by analysis to be most critical for the purpose at hand.

The most important step in developing a performance exercise is identifying the criterion, which usually involves a **task analysis**. Some major aspects of a task analysis are the following:

1. Developing a simulation that represents the entire performance as accurately as possible.
2. Specifying those elements in the task that are most relevant to the quality of performance. Some of these elements might be
   a. Speed of performance
   b. Accuracy of performance
   c. Number and seriousness of procedural errors
   d. Errors in following instructions
   e. Discrimination in selecting appropriate tools or equipment
   f. Economy of effort (amount of "lost motion")
   g. Timing (in the use of machinery or physical performances such as gymnastics)
   h. Intensity or force (in sports)
   i. Coherence and appropriateness of the sequence of steps followed
3. Selecting elements for observation or performance in proportion to their emphasis in instruction or training.
4. Establishing criteria and standards.
5. Evaluating these elements considering the conditions necessary to yield accurate, reliable, and valid measure.
6. Developing a reliable training program for rating and scoring.
7. Selecting those elements that require minimal time and expense.
8. Using results to (a) refine assessment and (b) improve the curriculum.
9. Providing feedback to relevant stakeholders in addition to students, such as parents, administrative personnel, and perhaps the community.

Selecting just the right task to assess the target behavior is absolutely crucial.

Criteria for Task Selection

Joan Herman, Pam Aschbacker, and Lynn Winters (1992) suggest six criteria to be used to evaluate assessment tasks:

- Match specific instructional intentions.
- Represent content and skills expected to be attained by students.
- Enable students to demonstrate their proficiencies and capabilities.
- Allow assessment of multiple goals.
- Reflect an authentic, real-world context.
- Allow an interdisciplinary approach.

All the criteria are important, but perhaps the greatest strength of performance assessment rests with the last two. Integrating a variety of skills (for example, completing a science experiment and writing an essay about it) is obviously more desirable than focusing on a single lower-level outcome. Credibility, which in turn influences student motivation, also will be enhanced if the task has at least "face validity" for real-world challenges.

In summary, developing a performance assessment is similar to developing any measurement, and includes the following steps:

1. Analyze the desired performance.
2. Identify crucial and representative elements for observation.
3. Select an appropriate simulation situation.
4. Specify the sequence of tasks that incorporate these crucial elements.
5. Specify the materials needed by the examinee to accomplish the tasks.
6. Prepare directions for examinee.
7. Develop methods for recording results of data collection.
8. Analyze reliability and validity.

Service-Learning Activities and Performance Assessment

The following service-learning activities from an environmentally oriented curriculum are presented for two reasons. First, they illustrate how performance assessments could be created to evaluate the performances. Second, the activities illustrate how the "environmental awareness" theme can be carried out in different subject areas.

Students might

- Read/dramatize environmental stories to young children (English/Language Arts).
- Write and publish books of environmental stories for their peers or younger students or perhaps special students (English/Language Arts).
- Create environmental stories and put on tape or in braille form for blind students (English/Language Arts).
- Collect and refurbish children's toys, donate and deliver them, and play with children (Family Studies).
- Plant a garden at a local park, on school grounds, at a nursing home, or at a shelter using compost and other environmentally friendly products (Science).
- Teach environmentally friendly songs to young children (Music).
- Recycle tools (e.g., teach nursing home residents to use them) and household items by cleaning up, fixing, and giving them to shelters (Technology Education).
- Teach younger students or nursing home residents how to e-mail or access the World Wide Web (Technology Education).
- Conduct a recycling project with younger students (Science).

- Sponsor, host, and generate data from a community- or school-wide recycling program (Math).
- Clean statues/outdoor artwork in parks (Art).
- Sponsor and teach an environmentally friendly hiking/camp session at a local elementary school (Health/Physical Education).
- Teach English as a Second Language (ESOL) students about the importance of recycling (Foreign Language).

In evaluating any of these performances, an assessment requires creating rubrics. In addition, most also have a knowledge component that could be evaluated with objective short-answer measures.

Portfolio Assessment

A particularly useful performance assessment type involves collecting and evaluating student work in a portfolio, not unlike that of a photographer or architect. Although used primarily in elementary school (in language arts), portfolios are used in middle school math and high school social studies and science, among others. Portfolios are also used at the college and university level—for example, a teacher's performance portfolio is useful when the teacher is seeking a job.

Judith Arter and Vicki Spandel (1992) have defined a student portfolio as a "purposeful collection of student work that tells the story of the student's efforts, progress, or achievement in (a) given area(s). This collection must include student participation in selection of portfolio content; the guidelines for selection; the criteria for judging merit; and evidence of student self-reflection" (p. 36). The systematic use of portfolios is a natural outgrowth of the educator's desire to cast a more humane perspective on how we evaluate and to diversify the methods so that we get a better match with instruction. Make no mistake, portfolios are messy to use, at times costly in time and effort, and potentially suffer from a serious problem of reliability of scoring. What are some reasons, however, to use this particular form of data collection?

Advantages of Portfolio Assessment

Among the more important reasons for using portfolios are that the portfolio

- is collected by the student in his or her own classroom, making it more natural;
- provides a vehicle for the student to exhibit achievements that have relevance for him or her, teachers, and especially parents;
- provides opportunity to track progress and growth over semester or year and to demonstrate a final level of performance;
- puts the student at the center of the instructional process;
- stimulates teachers to confer with both student and parent;
- enhances student self-evaluative skills and allows realistic assessment of proficiency;
- provides an ongoing picture of performance with a series of snapshots that are spliced into a progress film;
- represents tasks that are realistic approximations of everyday academic and real-world demands; and
- provides students the opportunity to "own" a piece of their learning: It is tangible evidence that, "I have accomplished something."

Types of Portfolios

But what kinds of materials should go into a portfolio? Literally anything that teacher and student together deem relevant. A list of the specific documents and exhibits is not unlike one generated for performance assessments in general and includes the following:

- Art projects
- Essays
- Journal entries
- Parent/teacher comments
- Posters
- Research papers
- Stories

- Attitude data
- Interviews
- Letters
- Poetry
- Problem solutions
- Self-assessments
- Test results

The listing is endless and can be lengthened with student and teacher creativity. Keep the requirements simple and share your criteria with the student.

Organizing a Portfolio System

As previously noted, the ideas of portfolios is not new-like so many performance assessments described earlier in this chapter, we have been using them since the beginning of humankind. Jim Popham (1995, p. 167–171) listed seven key elements in classroom portfolio assessment:

1. Develop student "ownership" in the portfolio by involving him or her in the selection and evaluation process.
2. Specify a variety of materials to be included.
3. Systematically collect and store the exhibits.
4. Identify the criteria for inclusion in the portfolio and evaluating the contents.
5. Require students to evaluate their portfolios periodically, with special emphasis on change, growth, gain, and progress.
6. Systematically schedule student portfolio evaluation conferences.
7. Involve parents in the portfolio process by informing them of the purpose and content and eventually showing them examples and samples.

In summary, the major advantage of using portfolios as performance assessments is the involvement and investment of the student in a process that directly relates to instruction. The disadvantage is the time and effort needed to create scoring rubrics (see previous section) and apply them systematically.

It is hoped that this chapter contained lots of assessment food for thought. The academic link in service-learning is the most important. Yes, sentiments and attitudes, particularly as they relate to character education, are important, but children are in school to learn. Let's teach them and then assess them in the best ways possible.

Referenceography

American Psychological Association, American Educational Research Association, and National Council on Measurement in Education (1999). *Standards for educational and psychological testing*. Washington, DC: American Educational Research Association.

Arter, J. A., & Spandel, V. (1992). Using portfolios of student work in instruction and assessment. *Educational Measurement: Issues and practice*, 11(1), 36–44.

Haladyna, T. H. (1997). *Writing test items to evaluate higher-order thinking*. Boston: Allyn & Bacon.

Herman, J. L., Aschbacker, P. R., & Winters, L. (1992). *A practical guide to alternative assessment*. Alexandria, VA: Association for Supervision and Curriculum Development.

Impara, J. C., & Plake, B. S. (Eds.) (1998). *The thirteenth mental measurements yearbook*. Lincoln: University of Nebraska Press.

Johnson, N. J., & Rose, L. M. (1997). *Portfolios-Classifying, constructing, and enhancing*. Lancaster, PA: Technomics.

Keyser, D. J., & Sweetland, R. C. (Eds.) (1988). *Test critiques* (Second Edition). Kansas City, MO: Test Corporation of America.

Linn, R. L., & Gronlund, N. E. (1995). *Measurement and assessment in teaching*. Englewood Cliffs, NJ: Merrill.

Payne, D. A. (1997). *Applied educational assessment*. Belmont, CA: Wadsworth.

Popham, W. J. (1995). *Classroom assessment: What teachers need to know*. Boston: Allyn & Bacon.

Samuda, R. J. (1998). *Psychological testing of American minorities*. Thousand Oaks, CA: Sage.

Stiggins, R. J. (1987). Design and development of performance assessments. *Educational Measurement: Issues and practice*, 6(3), 33–42.

Case Study

Reading instruction is a major component of every primary school curriculum. This was definitely the case at Nurture Primary School (NPS). A statewide initiative, which included a competitive grant application program, was in place to improve reading proficiency. In NPS reading and writing were emphasized everywhere and tied to all subject areas. As part of and in preparation for service-learning activities, reading relevant literature, creating memory books for Pine Manor residents, and reading to and being read to by residents were all part of the program. An example of relevant literature is an absolutely delightful story by Mem Fox titled "Wilfrid Gordon McDonald Partridge." It is a story about memory, what it means to the elderly in general, and a specific lady in particular, and how a child helped her find it again.

> **THOUGHT QUESTION**
> This is a really tough task, how to measure reading achievement. There are many commercial standardized, and some informal, reading achievement measures on vendors' shelves. Picking the right one is a challenge. You might want to review the sources of information about how to select standardized tests discussed earlier in this chapter. One of the immediate problems is, of course, the level of students involved here—first and second graders. Don't forget time to administer and costs.

Too many choices! Among those tests that stand out as possibilities are: Gray Oral Reading Tests (Third Edition) (PRO-ED, Inc.); *Basic Reading Inventory* (Fifth Edition) (Kendall/Hunt Publishing Co.); *Stanford Diagnostic Reading Test* (Fourth Edition) (Harcourt Brace Educational Measurement); *The Brigance Diagnostic Inventory of Basic Skills* (Curriculum Associates, Inc.); *Gates-McKillop-Horowitz Reading Diagnostic Tests* (Teachers College Press); *Metropolitan Reading Instructional Tests* (The Psychological Corporation); *Prescriptive Reading Mastery Inventory* (CTB/McGraw-Hill); and *Woodcock Reading Mastery Tests-Revised*

(American Guidance Service). Many possibilities were included so the reader might see the variety of choices that exist. One must be very careful. This would be a good opportunity to use a committee to give the "possibilities" intense screening.

The decision about how to measure reading achievement fortuitously was made for us. The State Department of Education, in cooperation with the faculty of a local elementary school, created the *Basic Literacy Test* (BLT) to use state-wide in assessing a variety of reading initiatives. The BLT covers kindergarten through fifth grade and contains the following sections:

Kindergarten Basics (9 points)
Knowledge about letters and ability to write name, identify eight basic colors, and tell age.

Phonics (24 points)
Letter recognition and sounds, read rhyming words, sound out short, long vowel words, r-controlled words, blends, digraphs, diphthongs, and two-syllable words.

Basic Sight Words (22 points)
Automatic recognition from Dolch list.

Oral Reading and Comprehension (45 points)
Twelve reading placement categories (instructional level) from preprimer through grade five. Child reads standard story aloud and answers comprehensive questions.

Don't forget that Evaluation Question Three required reading achievement data to be collected from both service-learning and non-service-learning students.

Five

Evaluating Writing Samples

One of the most popular and efficient methods to use in gathering information about the impact of service-learning activities is to evaluate student writing samples. One of the valuable things about using writing samples, in the form of essays, research papers, or journals, is that they can be linked to either the academic or service component of the activity. Content analyses, for example, can be used to check a procedure used to assess water quality in a local stream or examine opinions about helping the local humane society place lost or abandoned animals.

One example of analysis of writing samples used to evaluate a service-learning program has been reported by Dr. Robert Shumer of the Department of Work, Community, and Family Education at the University of Minnesota. In an unpublished 1996 document, Dr. Shumer reports on a creative writing course offered to juniors and seniors at a rural high school in Blue Earth, Minnesota. Two writing assignments were based on the students' service experience where they interviewed senior citizens in the community and then wrote stories for publication about senior partners. Seniors shared personal information about themselves and gained perspective on the developmental/growing process. Statistically significant quality differences were found between the papers of service-learning students and non-service-learning students. Interviews and questionnaires also revealed that teachers and students spent more time on the "service essays" because they were going to be published. There was more editing and rewriting, and students were more motivated. "The teacher was compelled to literally do more teaching, thus producing better overall writing."

Most teachers agree that scoring essay items and questions and evaluating writing samples are among the most time-consuming and frustrating tasks associated with conscientious classroom assessment. Teachers are frequently unwilling to set aside the large chunks of time necessary to score a stack of "blue books" carefully. It goes almost without saying that if scoring is to be reliable, teachers must expend considerable time and effort.

Before turning to specific methods of scoring, several general comments are in order. First, it is critical that the instructor prepare in advance a detailed "ideal" answer and identify some model papers that can be culled from those submitted. This answer and model responses will serve as the criterion by which each student's answer is judged. If this is not done, the results could be disastrous. The teacher's subjectivity could seriously inhibit consistent scoring, and student responses themselves might affect the evaluation of subsequent responses. Second, student papers should be scored anonymously, and all the answers to a given item should be scored at one time, rather than grading each student's total test separately.

Some general suggestions for evaluating student writing samples are presented in figure 5.1; most of them are commonsense.

The mechanics of scoring generally take different forms, depending on whether the focus is on content or subject matter or on delivery-that is, a unique communication consistent with accepted standards for expression, style, and grammar.

Evaluating Responses to Writing Prompts

Table 5.1 contains an outline of possible approaches to evaluation of writing samples. In a sense they describe the kinds of scoring rubrics that can be created, depending on the desired information wanted by the teacher or evaluator.

Figure 5.1 General Suggestions for Constructing and Evaluating Writing Samples

1. Limit the prompt so that it will have an unequivocal meaning to most students.

2. Use words that will convey clear meaning to the student.

3. Prepare enough questions to sample the material of the course broadly within a reasonable time limit.

4. Use writing samples for the purposes they serve-that is, to allow the students to demonstrate their ability to organize, handle complicated ideas, and create and express.

5. Prepare prompts that require considerable thought, but that can be answered in relatively few words.

6. Determine in advance how much weight will be accorded each of the various elements expected in a complete answer or work with other teachers to create scoring rubrics.

7. Without knowledge of students' names, score each question for all students. Use several scores and scorers if possible.

8. Require all students to answer all question on the test (this is important if the focus is on knowledge).

9. Write prompts about materials immediately germane to the course, experience, or activity.

10. Study past responses to determine how students performed.

11. Make gross judgments of the relative excellence of answers as a first step in grading.

12. Make word prompts as simple as possible to make the task clear.

13. Do not judge papers on the basis of external factors unless they have been clearly stipulated.

14. Do not make a generalized estimate of an entire paper's worth.

Table 5.1 Combinations of Writing Sample Scoring Methods and Focus Dimensions

	Focus Dimension	
Scoring Method	Content (Subject Matter)	Communication (Mechanics of Expression)
Holistic	Global overall evaluation	Global overall evaluation
Modified Holistic	Limited number of objectives	Limited number of objectives
Analytic	Checklist point scoring of content	Detailed critique of essay

Scoring Methods

Following is a brief description and discussion of these methods.

Holistic Scoring for Content Knowledge or Communication Effectiveness

In using this method, experienced readers make gross judgments about the quality of a given paper. The judgments are reported in two or more evaluation categories (for example, acceptable/unacceptable; A/B/C/D/F; inadequate/minimal/good/very good). As many as eight categories can be used. Comments sometimes accompany the feedback to writers. Such a procedure, if not done anonymously, can be very susceptible to "halo" rating errors. As described here, the holistic scoring approach usually focuses on assessing writing effectiveness. The method can be applied in evaluating content achievement, but probably with considerably less reliability. The holistic approach also lacks detailed diagnostic value unless it contains extensive comments, in which case it becomes almost analytic.

Modified Holistic Scoring for Communication Effectiveness

This method involves making overall evaluations of a limited number of components. Each component then gets a score of from 1 to 4, 5, or 6. The modified holistic method is efficient when numerous papers must be scored and multiple readers are being used. Training in the use of rubrics is the key to success. See figure 5.2 for an example of a modified holistic scoring rubric.

Modified Holistic Scoring for Content Knowledge

In reality, the modified holistic approach to scoring writing samples for content knowledge is probably used very little. If applied in its fullest form, it would involve a rater making judgments about the adequacy of knowledge a student exhibited about a limited number of objectives. For example, the teacher of a human anatomy and physiology class might present students with a task requiring them to describe the following major systems: skeletal, reproductive, digestive, circulatory, and urinary. Judgments would be made about the adequacy of each description. The analysis of responses would be more detailed than holistic, but less than analytic scorings.

Analytic Scoring for Communication Effectiveness

This method involves evaluating a number of specific categories- generally fewer than ten. Qualitative judgments are then made within categories. This method emphasizes the totality or "wholeness" of the response and is used when the instructor is focusing on expression rather than content. Rating methods are generally efficient, but their reliability is very much tied to the number of categories and subdivisions within categories. The categories chosen are usually determined by the "ideal" answer constructed by the teacher. Another useful approach is to use a standard set of categories, particularly if one's primary interest is in evaluating English composition.

The ultimate essay critique, however, is the detailed analysis paragraph by paragraph, line by line, and word by word-that is, the old red pencil approach. This type of analysis provides the maximum benefit to the student, but it obviously takes a great deal of time and effort.

Analytic Scoring for Content Achievement

The term **content achievement** as used here usually means knowledge and understanding. The analytic-or the Checklist Point Score-method involves partitioning the "ideal" response into a series of points or features, each of which is specifically defined. This scoring technique is particularly useful when content is to be emphasized over expression. Each element in the answer is identified and a credit value is attached to it. If possible, the instructor's table of specifications should be used as a guide for determining credits.

Consider the following restricted-response question: "What are the principal reasons that research in the social sciences has not progressed as far as has research in the biological and

---

**Figure 5.2   Modified Holistic Scoring Rubric for
                Evaluating Communication Effectiveness**

Scoring Dimensions, Definitions, and Components

Content Organization: The writer establishes the controlling idea through examples, illustrations, and facts or details. There is evidence of a sense of order that is clear and relevant.
- Clearly established controlling idea
- Clearly developed supporting ideas
- Sufficiently relevant supporting ideas
- Clearly discernible order of presentation
- Logical transitions and flow of ideas
- Sense of completeness

Style: The writer controls language to establish his/her individuality.
- Concrete images and descriptive language
- Easily readable
- Varied sentence patterns
- Appropriate tone for topic, audience, and purpose

Sentence Formation: The writer forms effective sentences.
- Appropriate end punctuation
- Complete sentences or functional
  fragments
- Appropriate coordination and/or subordination

Usage: The writer uses standard American English.
- Clear pronoun references
- Correct subject-verb agreement
- Standard form of verbs and nouns
- Correct word choice

Mechanics:
- Appropriate capitalization
- Appropriate internal punctuation
- Appropriate formatting
- Correct spelling

Score Point 1: The writing is **Inadequate**. Very few if any of the components for the dimension are demonstrated.
Score Point 2: The writing is **Minimal**. Some of the components for the dimension are demonstrated.
Score Point 3: The writing is **Good**, yet not exceptional. Many of the components are demonstrated, and they are demonstrated successfully.
Score Point 4: The writing is **Very Good**. Most of the components are demonstrated, and they are demonstrated consistently.

---

physical sciences?" The instructor's ideal answer might be, "Since the social scientist is himself part of what he is attempting to study, he cannot achieve the objectivity possible in the more precise sciences. Further, the conclusions he reaches frequently run counter to deeply held prejudices and are therefore unacceptable. Feeling that many of the social affairs of men are not susceptible to scientific study, people have been less willing to subsidize social research than medicine, for example. Finally, the scientific study of nature has a much longer history than the scientific study of man. This history has provided a much larger body of data and theory from which to progress."

The essential elements in this ideal answer are identified and quantitative weights are assigned to each. The checklist point score sheet might look something like this:

Element of Answer	Possible Points
1. Scientist part of his subject	2
2. Prejudice	3
3. Lack of financial support	2
4. Short history	1
5. Small body of facts and theory	1
6. Organization	1
7. Language usage	1

This approach to scoring has several advantages. It is objective and likely to be reliable. An analysis of the instructor's ideal response quite frequently reveals that the original question needs to be recast to elicit the desired response, which can result in time limit readjustment. A final advantage of the checklist point score method is its reliability. If used conscientiously, the analytic method can yield consistent scores on restricted-response essay items for different graders.

The difference between analytic and modified holistic is perhaps more a matter of degree than kind of scoring because both involve making general judgments. Writing samples can obviously undergo content analyses for opinions. Examples of this will be treated in the section Opinionnaire and Free-Response Methods in chapter 6.

Developing Scoring Rubrics

Scoring rubrics generally can be classified into three types: (a) holistic versus analytic, (b) developmental versus quantitative, and (c) generalized versus specific. Creating scoring rubrics for content (knowledge) appraisal, performance, communication effectiveness, or opinions requires considerable time and energy. Collaboration among teachers during the developmental stages of these rubrics can be very helpful.

Important terms in rubric creation and use are as follows:

- **Holistic.** A general overall gross judgment is made about a performance. A limited number of categories are predefined. Holistic rubrics usually have competency labels associated with them—for example, proficient, advanced, and so on.

- **Analytic.** A relatively detailed set of criteria is applied, usually after a holistic evaluation has been made. A compromise between holistic and analytic scoring is sometimes termed modified holistic.

- **Developmental.** These rubrics are created to span grade levels or "distance" on a competency continuum.

- **Quantitative.** A rating scale, usually in the form of anchored or "defined" numbers, is applied holistically or analytically.

- **Generalizable.** The same set of criteria categories is developed to be applied across different tasks. Holistic rubrics tend also to be generalizable.

- **Specific.** A rubric is created to score a single specific task. This approach is often used with open-ended supply and short-answer questions.

The most frequently used rubrics types are those that are holistic and generalizable and modified holistic, which is developmental. The Wisconsin Student Assessment System employs a holistic rubric, which in turn is modified slightly as it is applied to performance assessments in different subject areas. This system uses six categories as follows: Advanced Response, Proficient Response, Nearly Proficient Response, Minimal Response, Attempted Response, and Not Scorable. Following is an example at the general level, then illustrations of it applied in mathematics. The guidelines are for a Proficient Response.

> **General:** The response addresses all aspects of the task. It shows full application or appropriate knowledge and skills and uses methods of communication that are appropriate to the subject area and task. The response is conceptually and mechanically complete, although an occasional minor technical error may be present.

> **Mathematics:** The response completely addresses all aspects of the task. It includes
> _____ appropriate application of mathematical concepts and structures;
> _____ evidence of the use of appropriate mathematical procedures;
> _____ coherent use of mathematical words, symbols, or other visual representations that are appropriate to the task; and
> _____ logical conclusions based on known facts, properties, and relationships.

An effective rubric is developmental in nature and should have implications for instruction. Each level of the rubric should lead logically to the next (either above or below). The rubric should provide meaningful direction and feedback to the learner, thereby allowing the teacher to monitor both individual student and class progress.

After those long hours developing your scoring rubric, one final task is to pass it through a "quality filter" such as that included in figure 5.3. Attention to these criteria can help avoid problems during development, tryout, and training of scorers.

Figure 5.3 Checklist for Effective Rubrics*

_____ Describe full range of knowledge or skill (continuum)
_____ Provide examples
_____ Specify criteria for performance
_____ Minimize use of "missing skills" to define levels
_____ Use student-parent-appropriate language
_____ Use absolute-level criteria (vs. relative) to define performance where possible
_____ Use even number (at least four) of levels
_____ Maintain consistency in measurements reported (e.g., numbers, letters, adjectives)
_____ Have at least one level above "standard" for differentiation
_____ Don't use adjectives alone to differentiate levels
_____ Avoid levels/language that are too general or specific
_____ Try to keep "distance" between levels as equivalent as possible
_____ Represent distinct levels or degrees of performance
_____ Levels should reflect real-world differences

*Based on ideas contained in _Effective Scoring Rubrics–A Guide to Their Development and Use_ (1995). Springfield, IL: Illinois State Board of Education, School and Student Assessment Section.

Rubric Scoring a Science Performance Assessment

The following illustrative science performance assessment task* is taken from a pilot test with eleventh-grade high school students in the state of Georgia.

Performance Task

Explain the behavior of a red blood cell when

a. The cell is in pure water and
b. The cell is in a 30 percent salt solution.

Your explanation should include homeostasis, selective permeability, equilibrium, osmosis, and passive transport.

Students were required to respond on a specified precoded answer folder.

Content Context

The following background provided a framework for creating the scoring rubric:

Homeostasis is the process of maintaining a relatively constant internal environment despite changing external conditions. In a normal situation, the concentration of dissolved substances inside and outside the red blood cell is the same; therefore, the cell is isotonic to the outside environment (plasma). In this state of equilibrium, water is moving in and out of the cell at an equal rate.

In a hypertonic state, such as the cell being in pure water, there is a higher concentration of dissolved substances (a lower concentration of water) inside the cell. In this situation osmosis will occur. Water molecules will move through the cell's selectively permeable membrane from the area of higher concentration of water to lower (this is diffusion, the movement of water from the area of hypotonicity to the area of hypertonicity). Therefore, water will enter the cell more quickly than it is removed. Osmosis will continue in an attempt to reestablish equilibrium (isotonicity). The increase in osmotic pressure in the cell will change the cell's shape. Eventually, this pressure will cause the cell to burst or lyse. This passage of water through the membrane is an act of passive transport and requires no expenditure of energy by the cell.

In a hypotonic state, the opposite situation exists. The concentration of dissolved substances is higher outside the cell (the concentration of water is higher inside the cell). Therefore, water will move out of the cell more quickly than it enters. This is again an example of osmosis and is an act of passive transport. However, in this situation the osmotic pressure in the cell decreases and the cell shrinks or crenates.

Scoring Criteria and Rubric

The student responses were scored holistically with the following rubric:

- **Level 1.** A failed attempt. The student does not show an understanding of the processes involved. The information given is incorrect or confusing.
- **Level 2.** The student's explanation is limited. A general understanding of one or two processes is shown.

- **Level 3.** The student gives a partially developed, mostly general explanation of the behavior of the cell. The response may only explain one of the states, or both states are explained but the explanation of the conditions is reversed.

*Appreciation is expressed to Dr. Michael Bunch of Measurement, Incorporated, in Durham, North Carolina, for providing information in this section.

- **Level 4.** The student gives a somewhat specific explanation of the behavior of the cell in both states. A specific understanding of some of the processes is shown.

- **Level 5.** In this well-elaborated explanation of the behavior of the cell in both states, the student shows a mostly specific understanding of most of the processes involved.

- **Level 6.** The student gives a fully elaborated explanation of the behavior of the cell in both states. The discussion shows a strong, specific understanding of all the processes involved.

Sample Responses

Following are representative student responses for each of the six score levels.

- **Level 1.** When a red blood cell is in pure water, it does not float on the top. When a red blood cell is in a 30 percent salt solution, it does float on the top.

- **Level 2.** The behavior of a red blood cell when you put it in pure water is that it engorges with the water; then bursts like a balloon. When you put the blood cell in a 30 percent salt solution, the blood cell shrinks up until it's like a prune.

- **Level 3.** When homeostasis occurs in salt water, the red blood cell's selective permeability because of the salt water will expand trying to reach equilibrium with the salt water.

  A red blood cell in pure water will engage in osmosis having passive transport, meaning for 1 L of water coming into the cell, 1 L comes out of the cell. In the salt water the cell takes more water in than it lets out and in some cases will explode.

- **Level 4.** A cell of any type has selective permeability. Water can pass through any cell. If the cell is in pure water, osmosis will take place until it reaches equilibrium with the concentration gradient outside the cell. The cell has to maintain its homeostasis. It cannot get too hypertonic or too hypotonic. The cell may expand as it absorbs water until it reaches its equilibrium.

  Salt doesn't pass easily into a cell. The cell membrane is of selective permeability, so it may have to squeeze in. Again, if the cell is hypertonic it may strive for equilibrium. The salt may pass throughout the cell in passive transport. The salt may quickly pass out due to diffusion.

- **Level 5.** (A) When a red blood cell is in pure water, the selectively permeable membrane allows osmosis to occur. Water from outside the cell crosses the membrane and causes it to inflate and explode. This upsets the homeostasis and equilibrium of the red blood cell. (B) When a red blood cell is in a 30 percent salt solution, the effects of osmosis affect homeostasis, and the equilibrium in the cell is disturbed. The presence of the salt would probably forces water out of the cell and causes it to shrink and die.

(a) in pure water

(b) 30 percent salt solution

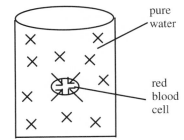

The water would cross the membrane of the red blood cell and cause it to eventually explode.

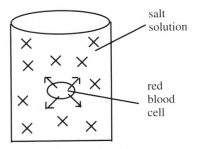

Water from inside the cell would cross the membrane to dilute the solution, and this would cause the cell to deflate, shrink, and die.

• **Level 6.** Cell reactions vary directly due to the mixture in which they are located. For instance, a red blood cell in hypotonic solution will swell inside, providing there is more pure water outside the cell. The pure water will travel to areas of lower concentration, thus inside the cell. Given time, the cell will explode due to lack of space between the walls. If the cell were in a hypertonic solution, the diffusion would take place by traveling to an area of lower concentration gradient. However, instead of swelling, the cell would shrink and shrivel, because salt is drier than water.

The process by which substances pass into and out of the cell is called osmosis. In natural conditions the cell can stop unnecessary substances from entering the cell. This is called selective permeability, and is controlled by homeostasis, the body's natural ability to strive toward equilibrium.

Passive transport is the equivalent of diffusion.

(A) Red blood cells are extremely important cells in the human body. If a red blood cell is placed in pure water, the environment around the cell has a direct effect on the cell. Red blood cells undergo homeostasis to regulate the environment around the cell and in the water. To maintain equilibrium, a red blood cell must regulate the amount of water being transported into the cell through osmosis. Because the water flows from an area of greater concentration to lesser concentration, the red blood cell eventually becomes saturated with water. Regulating devices normally control such situations, but if something goes wrong, the cell will burst.

(B) If a red blood cell is placed in a 30 percent salt solution, it once again undergoes homeostasis to regulate its environment. There would be a greater concentration of salt water around the cell into the salt water solution to hopefully regulate the concentration of salt to water. The cell eventually shrinks because of the loss of water.

For additional information about rubrics from conception to birth, see Taggart, Phifer, Nixon, and Wood (1998) and Popham (1997).

Rubrics can be applied to a variety of writing samples in addition to the obvious essay. Journals can be very revealing of both the knowledge acquired from a service-learning activity and feelings or attitudes about it. It is interesting for both teacher and student to sit and review previous and current writing samples. Both learn from the experience. Writing is a great way to reflect on a service-learning experience.

Referenceography

Popham, W. J. (1997). What's wrong-and what's right-with rubrics. *Educational Leadership*, 72–75.

Ruth, L., & Murphy, S. (1988). *Designing writing tasks for the assessment of writing*. Norwood, NJ: Ablex.

Taggart, G. L., Phifer, S. J., Nixon, S. A., & Wood, M. (1998). *Rubrics—A handbook for construction and use*. Lancaster, PA: Technomic.

White, E. M. (1994). *Teaching and assessing writing* (Second Edition). San Francisco: Jossey-Bass.

Case Study

Writing is an integral part of all instructional programs. The development of this proficiency is fundamental to successful academic progress. The development of writing skills is also integral to service-learning activities and projects. Students use writing as a major approach to **reflection**. They also frequently keep journals of their experiences. Obviously writing and research skills are used, for example, in language arts and social studies to learn about famous service-learning personalities such as Harriet Tubman, Albert Schweitzer, and Mother Teresa.

Although there were no formal evaluation objectives targeted at writing skills, as a matter of course two relevant assessments were made. The first was an attitude instrument focused on feelings about writing. This fifteen-item Agree-Disagree measure called "Do You Like to Write?" was used once in the fall and once in the spring. The second assessment was a formal rubric scoring of a narrative essay devoted to describing an instance where the author saw someone engage in an important service, or a time when the author did a personal service. The scoring rubric was one developed by the teachers of Wilkes County Primary School in Washington, Georgia. There are kindergarten, first- and second-grade versions of the writing checklist. Following is the grade two version. These evaluative categories link with the nine-stage developmental scoring scale that is used with state-wide assessments at grades three and five. It is important to study the terminology definitions before attempting to use the checklist. Note that at the bottom of the checklist an evaluation of the student's developmental writing ability is requested. Again, the potential user should study the nine-stage developmental scale attached before attempting to apply it to student writing samples. The kindergarten and first-grade versions of the checklist are presented in appendix C.

School _____
Grade _____
Teacher _____

Do You Like to Write?

Dear Student: Your teachers want to know how you feel about writing in school. The writing might be stories, recipes, reports or letters, or just anything that you make up. Please read (or have your teacher read) each of the following sentences about writing, then decide if you AGREE with what the sentence says or you DISAGREE with what the sentence says. Circle your choice for each sentence. Be sure to tell us how you really feel. There are no right or wrong answers.

1.	I really enjoy writing.	Agree	Disagree
2.	Very few students like to write.	Agree	Disagree
3.	Knowing how to write helps me in my other subjects.	Agree	Disagree
4.	Most of my classmates don't like to write.	Agree	Disagree
5.	I would rather write a story than study any subject.	Agree	Disagree
6.	I am not interested in writing.	Agree	Disagree
7.	Writing will help me all my life.	Agree	Disagree
8.	Only the best students can write.	Agree	Disagree
9.	Writing helps me think.	Agree	Disagree
10.	Writing is too much work.	Agree	Disagree
11.	Writing stories on the computer is really great fun.	Agree	Disagree
12.	I hate to write.	Agree	Disagree
13.	I write stuff at home.	Agree	Disagree
14.	I am writing more this year than I did last year.	Agree	Disagree
15.	There is a computer in my home.	YES	NO

WILKES COUNTY
Grade Two Writing Sample Assessment Checklist

Directions: Use the following Writing Benchmarks to assess the September & May writing assessment samples. Put a 0, 1, or 2 in each block. Remember, these Benchmarks reflect what a second-grade student should be able to do at the end of the year.

Student Name _____   Teacher _____   Year _____

Writing Topic: **Narrative Essay**	September	May
CONTENT Appropriate Title		
Sentences Relate to Topic		
Uses Details & Specific Examples		
ORGANIZATION Topic Sentence (beginning)		
Conclusion (end)		
STYLE Uses Descriptive & Elaborative Language		
GRAMMAR/MECHANICS Punctuation (sentence ending marks)		
Capitalization (beginning sentence)		
Complete Sentence		
Indentation		
Correct Spelling of Basic Sight Words		
Inventive Spelling		
Uses Capital Letters Appropriately (proper nouns, etc.)		
PENMANSHIP Legible (letter formation & spacing)		
TOTAL		

Marking Scale: 0 No, Never   1 Sometimes   2 Yes, Most of the Time

DEVELOPMENTAL STAGES (See attached sheet for description of each stage.)
Stage 1 ____   Stage 2 ____   Stage 3 ____   Stage 4 ____   Stage 5 ____   Stage 6 ____

September Total ____   May Total ____   IMPROVEMENT   NO IMPROVEMENT
                                                     (Circle One)

Wilkes County Georgia
Writing Sample Assessment Checklist Terminology
Second Grade

CONTENT

Appropriate Title—Title matches topic given, is separate from story, is clearly identifiable as a title, and is the actual name given to the story.

Sentences Relate to Topic—All sentences of the story relate to the topic. (If the story is written using good sentences, etc. but is not about topic, then all zeroes must be recorded.)

Uses Details & Specific Examples—Child writes details about the topic and gives specific examples about the details. Details contained within a picture or illustration drawn by the child to illustrate the story are not to be considered as a part of uses details & specific examples.

ORGANIZATION

Topic Sentence (beginning)—Child's story includes a topic sentence at the beginning.

Conclusion (end)—Child includes an ending sentence or sentences at the end of the story.

STYLE

Descriptive & Elaborative Language—Child uses descriptive and elaborative language.

GRAMMAR/MECHANICS

Punctuation (sentence ending marks)—Child uses periods and other appropriate ending punctuation marks, clearly exhibiting that child understands use of ending sentence punctuation.

Capitalization (beginning sentence)—Child uses capital letters at the beginning of complete sentences, showing knowledge of capitalization. Sentences end with periods; those begun with lower case "and," and then the word "I," are not sentences begun with a capital letter.

Complete Sentence—Child writes sentences that include a subject, verb, and object, beginning capital letter, and correct ending punctuation.

Indentation—Child indents the first word of first paragraph and the first word of any other paragraphs.

Correct Spelling of Basic Sight Words—Child spells basic sight words common to second graders. If the child spells any sight words incorrectly (even only two or three), a "1" must be recorded.

Inventive Spelling—Child uses inventive spelling of words not usually written by the average second grader. If no inventive spelling is present, a "0" must be recorded.

Uses Capital Letters Appropriately (proper nouns, etc.)—Child capitalizes proper nouns in sentences.

PENMANSHIP

Legible (spacing & formation)—Child's handwriting is legible. Letter formation and spacing of letters within words, and spacing between words are appropriate.

Marking Scale—Assign a "0," "1," or "2," only to the paper you are assessing. Do not decide if it's "yes," "sometimes," or "no" based on how the child has progressed, or what the child is doing in your classroom.

Developmental Stage—Determine the developmental stage. Use the description of stages on the attached sheet. Put the month and year next to the stage (e.g., Stage 1 3/00).

Developmental Stage/Scoring Guidelines
Georgia Writing Assessment

Stage 1: The Emerging Writer

Content ⟶ • Little or no topic development, organization, and/or detail.

Personal Expression ⟶ • Little awareness of audience or writing task.

Surface Features ⟶ • Errors in surface features prevent the reader from understanding the writer's message.

Stage 2: The Developing Writer

Content ⟶ • Topic beginning to be developed. Response contains the beginning of an organizational plan.

• Limited awareness of audience and/or task.

Personal Expression ⟶ • Simple word choice and sentence patterns.

Surface Features ⟶ • Errors in surface features interfere with communication.

Stage 3: The Focusing Writer

Content ⟶ • Topic clear even though development is incomplete. Plan apparent although ideas are loosely organized.

• Sense of audience or task.

Personal Expression ⟶ • Minimal variety of vocabulary and sentence patterns.

Surface Features ⟶ • Errors in surface features interrupt the flow of communication.

Stage 4: The Experimenting Writer

Content ⟶ • Topic clear and developed; development may be uneven. Clear plan with beginning, middle, and end. Beginning or ending may be clumsy.

• Written for an audience.

Personal Expression ⟶ • Experiments with language and sentence patterns. Word combinations and word choice may be novel.

Surface Features ⟶ • Errors in surface features may interrupt the flow of communication.

Stage 5: The Engaging Writer

Content ⟶ • Topic well developed. Clear beginning, middle, and end. Organization sustains the writer's purpose.

• Engages the reader

Personal Expression ⟶ • Effective use of varied language and sentence patterns.

Surface Features ⟶ • Errors in surface features do not interfere with meaning.

Stage 6: The Extending Writer

Content ⟶ • Topic fully elaborated with rich details. Organization sustains writer's purpose and moves reader through the piece.

• Engages and sustains reader's interest.

Personal Expression ⟶ • Creative and novel use of language and effective use of varied sentence patterns.

Surface Features ⟶ • Errors in surface features do not interfere with meaning.

Six

Evaluating Service-Learning Sentiments, Opinions, and Attitudes

An old fashioned term, **sentiments** (Nunnally, 1978), is being used here to describe interests, attitudes, values, likes, dislikes, personal reactions, dispositions, or preferences. In general, the focus is on how people feel about activities, events, experiences, people, products, places, and the like. One makes responses about sentiments when he or she (a) rank orders types of books to read during leisure time, (b) rates the perceived value of visiting and working with younger students on a like-dislike scale, or (c) prefers to help younger students read rather than go to a movie. Sentiments are feelings, but they also have some cognitive component.

Interests are preferences for particular experiences, events, or activities—e.g., I would rather work in the school garden than ride my bike, or I prefer to work outside than inside. Values, on the other hand, concern life goals and ways of living. Sample statements might be, "Service to others is more important to me than personal ambition," "I consider it more important to have people respect me than to like me," and "A person's duty to family comes before duty to society." Attitudes about feelings about targeted social or physical objects, organizations, whether type/groups of people or specific people, or issues and policies. Those feelings motivate one to respond or act in a particular way toward the "target." Sample statements that could be rated by an individual indicating the nature and intensity of attitude are, "All public schools should be integrated," "Old people should stay at home," and "Helping those less fortunate makes me feel good."

Creating Statements for Self-Report Affective Measures

General guidelines and criteria are crucial to the development of statements for affective measures. Obviously, the statements themselves are of critical importance. All the sophisticated analytic techniques in the world will not overcome an inferior statement that does not communicate. Following is a list of informal criteria for development and editing statements. **AVOID** statements that

- Refer to the past or future rather than to the present.
- Are factual or capable of being interpreted as factual.
- May be interpreted in more than one way.
- Are irrelevant to the psychological object under consideration.
- Are likely to be endorsed by almost everyone or by almost no one.
- Do not reflect the entire range of the affectivity.
- Use language that is complex, ambiguous, obtuse, or indirect.
- Are too long (more than twenty words).
- Contain more than one complete thought.
- Contain universals such as *all*, *always*, *none*, and *never* because they often introduce ambiguity.
- Contain ambiguous words such as *only*, *just*, *merely*, and others of similar nature.
- Are formed with compound or complex sentences.
- Use words that may not be understood by those who are to be given the completed scale (readability).
- Use double negatives.

Most of these suggestions are commonsense and are based on the need to communicate. Some of the suggestions are similar to the suggestions for writing cognitive test questions, particularly true-false items.

Rating Scales

Rating methods are frequently used to record likes, preferences, and attitudes toward products, people, activities, experiences, or activities. Ratings might be self-report or used by an observer. They might be made about something the student has created or done. Rating scales might use a sequence of defined numbers (e.g., 5 = most pleasant . . .1 = most unpleasant), graphic stimuli with verbal description distributed along a straight line, or checklists. Verbally anchored scales usually call for one of three kinds of ratings: **Agreement**, **Evaluation**, or **Frequency**. For example:

Agreement: Education is the most important factor in living a productive life.
Strongly Agree   Agree   Uncertain   Disagree   Strongly Disagree

Frequency: I visit the school library.
Rarely   Sometimes   Frequently   Very Often

Evaluation: I would rate my ability to make friends as
Not Very Good   Average   Good   Excellent

There will always be a problem of interpretation of terms used in ratings scales. Be sure to use words that your respondents understand and check on objectivity by pilot testing and debriefing.

Figure 6.1 contains a sample attitude scale appropriate for high and middle school students related to feelings about service-learning experiences.

A Simplified Attitude Scale Construction Technique

Corey (1943) has described a relatively efficient method for constructing an attitude scale. The test development process itself can serve as a learning experience. Its steps are as follows:

1. **Collect a pool of statements.** Each student, for example, might be asked to write three or four statements representing various attitudes toward cheating. Illustrative statements might be:

    > Cheating is as bad as stealing.
    > If a test isn't fair, cheating is all right.
    > I won't copy, but I often let someone else look at my paper.
    > A little cheating on daily tests doesn't hurt.

2. **Select the best statements.** Using the criteria for constructing attitude statements described in the previous section, about fifty items might be culled from the initial pool of one hundred or one hundred fifty statements. Duplicates are eliminated, as are statements that are obviously ambiguous to the teacher or students. The students, for example, might be asked to indicate all those statements on the master list that represent opinions favoring cheating (with a plus sign) and those representing negative opinions about cheating (with a minus sign). An agreement criterion of 80 percent is suggested; a show of hands is an efficient way to gather these data.

**Figure 6.1   South Carolina Learn and Serve Survey
(High School and Middle School Form)**

Please circle the number that best describes your thoughts about each statement.

    6 = Strongly Agree   2 = Somewhat Disagree
    5 = Somewhat Agree   1 = Strongly Disagree
    4 = Agree   0 = Cannot Rate
    3 = Neutral

Service-Learning Activities:

1. Acquaint me with career possibilities.	0	1	2	3	4	5	6
2. Broaden my understanding of places and people.	0	1	2	3	4	5	6
3. Develop personal qualities in me such as confidence and self-reliance.	0	1	2	3	4	5	6
4. Help me acquire new skills, interests, and knowledge.	0	1	2	3	4	5	6
5. Help me form habits of community service and volunteerism.	0	1	2	3	4	5	6
6. Help me understand better what I study in class.	0	1	2	3	4	5	6
7. Give me an opportunity to be creative and see my ideas put to work.	0	1	2	3	4	5	6
8. Help me to understand better my community and how it works.	0	1	2	3	4	5	6
9. Teach me how to work better in a team.	0	1	2	3	4	5	6
10. Build school spirit.	0	1	2	3	4	5	6
11. Should be worked into all of my classes.	0	1	2	3	4	5	6
12. Make learning more interesting.	0	1	2	3	4	5	6
13. Help me to see how what I study is connected to my life outside of school.	0	1	2	3	4	5	6

3. **Administer the inventory.** The following directions might be used:
   Directions: This is not a test in the sense that any particular statement is right or wrong. All these sentences represent opinions that some people hold about cheating on tests. Indicate whether you agree or disagree with the statements by putting a plus sign before all those with which you agree and a minus sign before those with which you disagree. If you are uncertain, use a question mark. After you have gone through the entire list, go back and

draw a circle around the plus signs next to the statements with which you agree very strongly, and a circle around the minus signs next to the statements with which you disagree very strongly.

The inventory may be duplicated and distributed or administered orally. Discussion should be discouraged. Anonymous administration is preferable.

4. **Score the inventory.** Scoring may be accomplished by either teacher or student. The first step involves identifying those statements that were judged by the entire group (in Step 2) as favoring classroom cheating. Next, the following score values are applied: a plus sign with a circle receives five points; a plus sign alone, four points; a question mark, three points; a minus sign two points; and a minus sign, with a circle, one point. Thus, when a person disagrees very strongly with a statement that favors classroom cheating, that person earns one point; if that person agrees very strongly with the same statement, that person gets five points.

Those statements that express opposition to cheating are scored in the opposite fashion: a plus sign with a circle receives one point; a plus sign alone, two points; a question mark, three points; a minus sign, four points; and a minus sign with a circle, five points. In other words, a student who disagrees very strongly with a statement that opposes cheating actually has a very favorable attitude toward such a practice.

If the inventory contains fifty items, the maximum score possible is two hundred fifty, which indicates a favorable attitude. The minimum score possible is fifty, and an indifference score is in the neighborhood of one hundred fifty.

Service-learning programs and projects frequently require the collection of survey data from a variety of stakeholders and audiences. The use of well-constructed opinionnaires can facilitate efficient collection of data related to goals and objectives, needs, effectiveness of inservice programs, and general perceived program impact.

Goal Attainment Scaling

One of the problems contributing to inefficiency in instrumentation in evaluating service-learning activities and programs is the fact that different treatment/activity units within the same site sometimes have different goals or objectives because they may be starting from different levels. The goals or objectives may be personal development—e.g., to learn how to relate more effectively with adults or peers, or product-based—e.g., to develop landscaping or a horticulture greenhouse that will result in plants to be used in beautification projects. An assessment technique useful in collecting data under these conditions is **goal attainment scaling**.

Goal attainment scaling (GAS) historically has been used in a variety of mental health settings where individual patient or client goals need to be addressed. The best single source of information about the technique is contained in a book edited by Kiresuk, Smith, and Cardillo (1994). In a real sense, application of GAS involves standard setting before the implementation of treatment. Goals are negotiated between patient (student) and therapist (teacher/project director). There could be individual or group goals. Two illustrative goals are as follows:

Enhanced knowledge about issues related to water pollution
Value voluntary community service to senior citizens

Once consensus has been reached regarding the goals, indicators must be specified. Indicator data for the first goal, for example, were gathered from a forty-item teacher-made knowledge test. The second goal was assessed from archival data maintained by the project director. One of the singular advantages of this technique is that expectations are set on an individual

Table 6.1   Illustrations of Goal Attainment Scaling

Level of Attainment	Scale 1 Environmental Knowledge	Scale 2 Appreciation of Community Service
Much Less −2	Less than 4-point gain or loss	Attends 20% of sessions or less
Somewhat less −1 than expected	5–9-point gain	Attends 21–39% of sessions
Expected level 0 of outcome	10-point gain	Attends 40–60% of sessions
Somewhat more +1 than expected	11–15-point gain	Attends 61–79% of sessions
Much more +2 than expected	16 or more point gain	Attends 80% or more of sessions

basis, so you can adjust different starting positions. Table 6.1 contains an illustration of how this might be accomplished for our two sample goals. The Level of Attainment scale is fairly standard for GAS applications. Students, project coordinators, or other stakeholders determine the level of attainment. At the conclusion of the treatment, each goal can be evaluated and data aggregated for individuals or groups.

Opinionnaire and Free-Response Methods

The questionnaire survey is a frequently used polling method to gather opinion and attitude data. The term **opinionnaire**, as opposed to questionnaire, is actually used more frequently since it suggests an emphasis on feelings rather than facts. The use of a well-constructed opinionnaire tends to systematize the data-gathering process and help ensure that the relevant questions are asked and that all important aspects of the problem are surveyed.

The opinionnaire method, either open-ended or closed (structured), is frequently maligned. But as is often the case, it is the user who should be castigated for improper use or construction, not the method itself. If properly constructed and analyzed, opinionnaires can provide very valuable information about either cognitive or affective variables. They are, or can be, efficient with regard to time for construction and administration to large or small groups of respondents. They are also relatively inexpensive. They do require carefully crafted questions, however. The unstructured free-response opinionnaire requires large amounts of time for content analyses of the responses, and a great deal of subjectivity may be involved in interpreting these responses. Respondents may "wander around" in answering the questions, so evaluators should be prepared to separate the wheat from the chaff. Unfortunately, opinionnaires are often haphazardly constructed, without proper concern paid to the phrasing of questions, or the means of summarizing or analyzing the data. Pilot testing is frequently not conducted.

Six criteria for a "good" opinionnaire are as follows:

- Brevity.
- Including items of sufficient interest and "face appeal" to attract the attention of the respondent and cause him or her to become involved in the task.
- Provision for eliciting sufficient depth of response to avoid superficial replies.
- Wording questions to avoid being suggestive, unstimulating, or uninteresting, or offensive.
- Phrasing questions in such a way as to allay suspicion about hidden purposes and not to embarrass or threaten the respondent.
- Phrasing questions so that they are not too narrow in scope, allowing the respondent reasonable latitude in his or her responses.

Opinionnaires are generally of two types: the "closed" or precategorized type, and the "open" or free-response type. Rating scales are also frequently associated with the structured opinionnaires. The open-ended form of opinionnaire should be adopted for most uses unless many respondents are involved. The use of such free-response questions allows the evaluator to cover a wide variety of topics in an efficient manner. Analysis of the responses to free-response questions can be quite time consuming and difficult, however. In preparing opinionnaires, some general cautions should be observed:

- Spell out in advance the objectives, purposes, and specifications for the instrument. This task should be undertaken before questions are written.
- Try to limit the length of the opinionnaire (e.g., ten questions). If the respondent becomes impatient to finish, he or she is less likely to consider answers carefully.
- Make sure respondents understand the purpose of the opinionnaire and are convinced of the importance of responding completely and candidly.
- If possible, use a logically or temporarily related sequence of questions.
- Make sure respondents are motivated to answer questions thoughtfully.
- Control administration of the opinionnaire so as to prevent respondents from talking with one another about the questions before answering them.
- Urge respondents to express their own thoughts, not the responses they think the evaluator, teacher, principal, or project director wants.
- Be sure the directions are clear, definite, and complete.
- If possible, try out the opinionnaire with a couple of respondents to identify and clear up ambiguous questions, difficult terms, or unclear meanings.

Content Analysis

An evaluator will ordinarily undertake a content analysis of the responses to opinionnaire questions. Content analysis is a systematic, objective, and sometimes quantitative examination of free-response material. In addition to examining opinionnaire responses, content analyses of textbooks, television broadcasts, essays, records of interpersonal interactions, plays, stories, dramas, newspaper articles, speeches, or propaganda materials may be undertaken.

Several steps are involved in completing a content analysis.

1. **Identify the units for the purpose of recording results.** The specification of units, which requires great care, may be undertaken before beginning the analysis if the analyst knows what to expect, or after a sample of the responses has been examined. A unit is usually a single sentence, although any brief phrase that summarizes an idea, concept, feeling, or word will suffice.

2. **Identify the categories into which the units will be placed.** For example, the unit might be a sentence and the category a type of sentence—for example, declarative or interrogative.

3. **Analyze all the content (or a representative sample) relevant to the problem.** A given piece of material could be sampled for a given document (log, diary, etc.), or samples could be taken.

4. **Seek to attain a high degree of objectivity.** The analyst may want to finish an analysis or put it aside and redo it (or a portion of it) later to check agreement of results with the analyst or another reader. A comparison of the work of two analysts working independently could serve as another check on objectivity.

5. **Quantify the results, if at all possible.** The use of simple summary indices such as frequency counts and percentages can be very helpful.

6. **Include a sufficiently large number of samples to ensure reasonable reliability.** The larger the sample of material(s) analyzed, in general, the greater the reliability.

An Illustrative Content Analysis

In an effort to evaluate the impact on an eight-week summer enrichment program for academically and artistically talented students, the author asked several questions, such as the following, on a participant follow-up opinionnaire:

1. What contribution, if any, did the program make toward your developing a positive attitude toward learning?
2. How suitable were the instructional methods?
3. To what degree did the program influence your desire to attend college?
4. What do you feel were the most beneficial dimensions of the program?

A content analysis of the last question yielded the results Shown in table 6.2 (with a sample of fifty subjects).

Not only were relevant dimensions of the program identified, but a ranking of the importance of these dimensions also became possible. The fact that this information came from the participants themselves helps ensure the validity of the responses. If precategorized responses had been used, data might have been biased.

But not all data need to be gathered in paper-and-pencil form.

Table 6.2 Illustrative Content Analysis for Questions
"What do you feel were the most beneficial dimensions
of the program?"

	Frequency	Percent
a. Contact with individuals with both different and similar interests.	34	68
b. Freedom for independent and in-depth study.	12	24
c. The high quality of teachers.	9	18
d. The availability of cultural events, films, speakers, and the like.	8	16
e. Freedom to broaden interests.	5	10

Interviews and Focus Groups

One final set of data collection methods to be considered are interviews and focus groups. Long used in marketing research, interviewing and focus group methodology has recently gained wide acceptance in educational evaluation.

Brown (1994) has noted that the purpose of interviewing in qualitative evaluation is to find out what the program means to participants. Interview formats can very on a continuum from highly structured, evaluator-directed question and response guides to informal conversations whose focus and direction are guided by participants. Participant observation always includes conversational interviews because of the level of interaction between the evaluator and participants. The selection of interview format is determined by the type of information that is desired, the amount of time available to the evaluator to collect data, and the level of comparability of findings that is desired. The less structured interview formats require more time and are less comparable, but they allow participants to discuss issues and concerns that are of utmost importance to them. Evaluators must consider the trade-offs carefully when selecting interview formats.

Interviews can be with individuals or groups of participants. Each approach has advantages, and both can be included in a single evaluation design. Focus group interviewing is a form of qualitative data collection in which the evaluator functions as discussion facilitator for a small group of participants and relies on interaction within the group to provide insights about topics proposed by the evaluator. Krueger (1988) argues that focus group interviews can provide vital information on the impact of programs on participants. Morgan (1988) explores the advantages and disadvantages of focus group interviews.

Advantages of focus groups are:

- they are relatively easy to conduct,
- they require less time than multiple individual interviews,
- they provide the opportunity to collect data from group interaction, and
- they provide an opportunity for group discussion opinion formation of researcher- generated topics.

Weaknesses of focus group interviews are:

- they may not be conducted in a naturalistic setting,
- it is impossible to discern individuals' perspectives,
- the degree to which the presence of the evaluator and other participants affects responses of any individual cannot be determined,
- comparison of data across focus groups is difficult because group interaction determines the direction or focus of discussion, and
- fewer questions can be asked because more interviewees are involved.

In addition to format, the wording and sequencing of questions affect interviewee responses. Interview questions in qualitative evaluation should be singular, clearly worded, nonleading, and open-ended.

One of the most important goals of interviewing in evaluation is to find out *why* different individuals or different levels of persons construct different meanings about a program. In other words, to be able to say something about the reasons for different or conflicting findings about a program, data need to be generated that account for these differences in perspective or meaning. One of the most *ineffective* question formats is to ask "Why?" after other questions. Role playing and simulation questions or questions asking for descriptions or examples are superior techniques for finding out why participants function the way they do or have the perspectives they share about a program.

Interviewing as many participants as possible in different contexts and across times throughout the program will provide an understanding of evolving perspectives. Key informants are special people (e.g., a service-learning coordinator) in the social context with whom the evaluator spends more time than with other participants. The key informant provides insights and insider interpretations that the evaluator may not be able to access as an outsider to the group or situation. Key informants are selected because they may be particularly well informed about the program, may be available to the evaluator, may have played a key role in helping the evaluator gain access to the site, or other characteristics that make them special and different from other participants. Selection of a key informant who is peripheral to the social structure or who is viewed negatively by some or all of the program participants can be detrimental to the evaluation process.

If you are going to make informed decisions about how the program is going or what its impact was, then you need to gather the best information possible. That requires a lot of time and effort.

Referenceography

Berdie, D. R., Anderson, J. F., & Niebuhr, M. A. (1986). *Questionnaire design and use.* (Second Edition). Metuchen, NJ: Scarecrow Press, Inc.

Brown, M. J. M. (1994). Qualitative and ethnographic evaluation. In D. A. Payne *Designing educational project and program evaluations*, 121–141. Boston: Kluwer.

Converse, J. M., & Presser, J. (1986). *Survey questions-Handcrafting the standardized questionnaire.* Newbury Park, CA: Sage.

Corey, S. M. (1943). Measuring attitudes in the classroom. *Elementary School Journal*, 43, 437–461.

Hopkins, D. (1992). *A teacher's guide to classroom research.* Buckingham: Open University Press.

Kiresuk, T. J., Smith, A., & Cardillo, J. E. (Eds.) (1994). *Goal attainment scaling: Applications, theory, and measurement.* Hillsdale, NJ: Erlbaum.

Krueger, R. A. (1988). *Focus groups: A practical guide for applied research.* Newbury Park, CA: Sage.

Morgan, D. L. (1988). *Focus groups as qualitative research.* Newbury Park, CA: Sage.

Mueller, D. J. (1986). *Measuring social attitudes.* New York: Teachers College Press.

Nunnally, J. C. (1978). *Psychometric theory* (Second Edition). NY: McGraw-Hill.

Spector, P. E. (1992). *Summated rating scale construction.* Newbury Park, CA: Sage.

Case Study

Instrument development is both art and science. In the case of the current evaluation, perhaps more art because of the age of both the servicers and servicees.

Creating efficient and valid instrumentation is a major challenge for the evaluator. It would be unusual to be able to use an off-the-shelf instrument; most data collection devices must be created or at the very least adapted. There is a very large body of literature that contains relevant prototypic instrumentation. Resources were referenced at the end of chapters 4–6 and in appendix C (Sample Instrumentation).

Evaluation Objective One (attitude toward elderly), Two (attitude toward reading), Four (attitude toward service-learning), and Five (nursing home resident satisfaction) required the development of an affective inventory, survey form, or questionnaire.

THOUGHT QUESTION

If you are really motivated and were totally stimulated by the content of this chapter, try your hand at some instrument development. At least lean back and think about (cognitively monitor) how you might go about approaching the construction task.

Following are four instruments that were created for the project. The first, *Ideas about Young People and Older People*, was based on research reported by Kogan (*Research and Aging*, 1979) and Krouse and Chapin (*Gerontology and Geriatrics Education*, 1988). It is basically an intergenerational awareness scale. The "smiley faces" attitude toward reading scale was created for specific use in this project, as were the helping others survey and interview schedule (or self-report device) to be used with the seniors. Decisions about whether to use the attitude scale as an interview schedule or self-report device will depend on the ability of respondents to communicate and their comfort level with either approach.

Ideas About Young People and Older People

I am _____ a Boy.
_____ a Girl.
I am in _____ grade.

Directions (To be Read by Teacher):

First, place a check mark beside Boy or Girl and write in the grade you are in. I am going to read some statements that say something about children and older people. Think very hard and decide if you Agree with the statement, Disagree with the statement, or you Can't Decide. Just put an "X" (cross) through your choice.

For example:

Children and old people can get along together   Disagree   Can't Decide   Ag**X**ee

This student agreed with the statement that children and old people can get along together.

Here are some different statements:

1.	Old people only like to talk about the past.	Disagree	Can't Decide	Agree
2.	Old people are too tired to play games.	Disagree	Can't Decide	Agree
3.	Being young isn't easy.	Disagree	Can't Decide	Agree
4.	When they were growing up, old people didn't do the things I do.	Disagree	Can't Decide	Agree
5.	Children growing up in the older days had to work all the time.	Disagree	Can't Decide	Agree
6.	Children and old people don't get along because they are too different.	Disagree	Can't Decide	Agree
7.	When people get old they still want to learn about things.	Disagree	Can't Decide	Agree
8.	All children feel lonely sometimes.	Disagree	Can't Decide	Agree
9.	When you are old, you no longer have dreams of things to do.	Disagree	Can't Decide	Agree
10.	All old people are alike.	Disagree	Can't Decide	Agree
11.	Many old people still like to work.	Disagree	Can't Decide	Agree
12.	Young people can learn things from old people.	Disagree	Can't Decide	Agree
13.	Old people have nothing new to try.	Disagree	Can't Decide	Agree
14.	Old people mostly like to just sit and talk.	Disagree	Can't Decide	Agree
15.	Being young makes it easier to do everything.	Disagree	Can't Decide	Agree
16.	It's always sad to be old.	Disagree	Can't Decide	Agree
17.	Talking to yourself is a sign of old age	Disagree	Can't Decide	Agree
18.	Growing old is mostly just full of worries.	Disagree	Can't Decide	Agree

Attitude Toward Reading
(Prototype)

Directions Read to Student
Each statement below describes a feeling toward reading. The survey will help determine how you feel about reading. There is no right or wrong answer, and you will not be given a grade. Answer each statement as honestly as you can by circling the puppy that best describes how you feel about the statement.

                 Puppy 1 = Very Happy
                 Puppy 2 = Happy
                 Puppy 3 = Not happy or unhappy
                 Puppy 4 = Unhappy
                 Puppy 5 = Very Unhappy

1. How do you feel about getting a book for a present?

2. How do you feel when you are asked to read in class?

3. How do you feel about reading books for fun at home?

The score is the sum of the puppy ratings such that the higher the score, the more positive the attitude (i.e., happiest puppy = "5" if statement is positive, or "1" if negative, etc.).

Student Service Survey

I am _____ a Boy.
_____ a Girl.
I am in _____ grade.

Directions (To be Read by Teacher):

First, place a check mark beside Boy or Girl and write in the grade you are in.

Next, I am going to read some statements that say something about how boys and girls feel about helping others at Pine Tree Manor. After I read a sentence I want you to think about it and what it means to you. If you like what I said a lot, put an "X" on the face with the BIG SMILE. If you don't like what I read, put an "X" on the face with a FROWN. If you cannot decide, put an "X" on the face BETWEEN THE SMILE AND FROWN. I will call out the number of the sentence I am reading.

Let's practice one.

Practice Sentence: Birthdays are fun.   (X) (·) (·)

This student put an "X" on the BIG SMILE, meaning that he or she really like the sentence, "Birthdays are fun."

1. I like visiting Pine Tree Manor.

2. I think the people at Pine Tree Manor respect me.

3. I learned a lot going to Pine Tree Manor.

*4. When the weather is bad, I don't like to go to Pine Tree Manor.

5. Visiting older people makes me feel good.

6. Helping others is important.

7. What I learned at Pine Tree Manor will help me in the future.

*8. Older people can't teach you anything.

9. The people at Pine Tree Manor make me feel good.

10. I tell people about what I do at Pine Tree Manor.

11. I wish I could spend more time at Pine Tree Manor.

12. What I do at Pine Tree Manor makes school more fun.

*13. Sometimes going to Pine Tree Manor is fun; sometimes it's not.

*14. I don't feel good about asking older people questions about themselves.

*Reverse-scored items.

Survey of Pine Tree Manor Residents
(Self-Administered or Interview)

Please answer the following questions as completely and honestly as you can. If you need help, please ask.

1. What did you like MOST about having the students come to Pine Tree Manor this year?

2. What did you like LEAST about having the students come to Pine Tree Manor this year?

3. What would you change if the students come to Pine Tree Manor again next year?

4. What could the school do to make student visits more important to you?

Seven

Designing Data Collection Plans

Although service-learning activities in and of themselves have inherent value and merit, we are frequently called upon to demonstrate that merit. A systematic data collection design can help us do just that. The most important contribution evaluation can make is toward the **improvement** of the service-learning experience, activity, or program. Certain assumptions underlie the design of data collection plans.

Evaluation Tenets

All Evaluation Is Comparative

Benchmarks are needed to assist in interpreting evaluation results. These benchmarks may be **absolute** or **relative**. Absolute benchmarks are (a) created for evaluation purposes or (b) identified or aggregated from other sources. A group of "experts" may make judgments, for example, about what percentage of students should agree that their service experience was "Good" or "Outstanding" for the activity to be meritorious. This "percentage" then becomes a **standard**. In the other sense the word benchmark, data from existing records, files, archives, or normative data sets also can be used. The average "satisfaction" score for last year's partners is used to help interpret this year's evaluation data. The usual comparative data, in the relative sense, are collected concurrently with the service-learning data and contrasted. These topics will be treated in greater detail later in this chapter.

It is proposed that the term **contrast group** rather than **control group** be used in educational evaluation studies. This term simply refers to an existing or to-be-generated data set against which our "experimental" results are to be contrasted. In most educational evaluation situations we do not have the luxury of having very extensive control of subjects, or in some cases treatments for that matter. The use of the term **contrast group** is, therefore, more descriptive of the true state of affairs and tends to remove evaluations from the domain of the traditional experimental paradigm by recasting the nature and focus of the contrast.

The Design of Evaluation Studies Is Evolutionary

The fact that evaluations take place in naturally occurring settings can lead to significant design and implementation problems. Because the situation is natural—a school or classroom, for example—changes are always expected and experienced. The evaluation design must be flexible. What do I do about the "treatment teacher" who is going to be on maternity leave for six weeks? What do I do about the 50 percent student sample that was out with flu on the final data collection date? These and other frightening occurrences can cause an evaluator consternation. Of course, if you are not ready for catastrophes, then you shouldn't be an evaluator. Fortunately, a good design includes provisions for meeting unanticipated problems. Certain objectives may become unrealistic due to treatment failure or lack of availability of data and may require a change in criterion measures. Expect the unexpected!

The Complexity of Contemporary Evaluation Requires Multiple Models and Methods

The just noted change in criterion problems highlights the need for alternative data types and data sources. The marriage of quantitative and qualitative methods is in process (Reichardt & Rallis, 1994). Courtship is in progress, but the merger has not been consummated. The birth of mixed methods allows for greater responsiveness to evaluation questions, which in turn allows for greater responsiveness to stakeholder needs. The cross-fertilization of methods and philosophy allows for the fuller and richer assessment of an evaluation question. Triangulation (multiple methods, common target) is now the keystone in the evaluation arch that must support the weight of an innovative program or project (Serow, 1997).

Involve All Relevant Stakeholders in the Evaluation

We obviously will be gathering data from students, but don't forget the valuable contribution that can be made at the design and collection stage by teachers, partners, administrators, and parents. All have vested interest in the implementation of service-learning and the impact of the activities and experiences. Parents and teachers are *always* interested in the academic link in the service chain. The above groups can also help with interpretation.

Be Ever Watchful for Unintended Effects

Rarely are all our dreams fulfilled or our hypotheses confirmed. In a dynamic classroom or school many uncontrollable influences may distort or change our "treatment." Bias is everywhere, whether during implementation, in the instruments, or during collection. Observation and interviewing are the best ways to try to find that black cat on a moonless night in a darkened room. You will be surprised what you might find: "I feel so inadequate when I try to help these homeless people. I can't keep trying." Both individual and group revelations will be observed: "Discipline referrals to the principal's office were reduced by 38 percent!" This effect was attributed to a cross-age tutoring project, when in fact it was the result of a change in administrative policy that required teachers to deal with discipline problems at the classroom level first.

Evaluating service-learning involves some significant methodological challenges.

Methodological Problems in Evaluating Service-Learning Projects

Our public schools make a valiant effort to meet all students' needs: cognitive, affective and psychomotor. This is a virtually impossible task at best, at least with a "traditional" curriculum. Service-learning attempts to focus on many developmental needs of students and pre-adolescents. In addition to intellectual needs, service-learning addresses such needs as peer acceptance, creative self-expression, feelings of self-worth and personal competence, career exploration, capacity for responsible intimate relationships, management skill development, and independence. It has been conclusively demonstrated that intellectual, affective and hands-on service-learning experiences can help develop and reinforce fulfillment of these needs.

Each service-learning activity generally has a classroom link and service target. Outcomes are project-specific and based on needs analysis data. It is generally expected that service-learning projects will enhance (a) the mastery and retention of classroom learning objectives, (b) feelings of civic/school responsibility, (c) ties among school, parents, students, and the community, (d) student self-esteem, (e) student motivation, (f) interpersonal skills, and readiness for the world of work (Shumer, 1994).

The variety of possible outcomes in a single service-learning site poses problems for the evaluator faced with the task of presenting evidence of "overall" impact. The author is working with a service-learning project that involves five different teachers at five different grade levels. The projects involve cross-age tutoring, ornamental horticulture, senior citizen support, school service, and environmental protection. To top it all off, the majority of the service providers are special needs students. Since generalizability is not of paramount concern, it was decided to do five case studies (Merriam, 1988).

Problems in Implementing Service-Learning Projects

Evaluation efforts may be complicated by the fact that sometimes different, distant, and distinct sites are involved in implementing decentralized service concepts. Diversity of clientele and the multisite nature of the operation can have both positive and negative implications for evaluation. On the one hand, having different sites suggests that replications of a given approach to service could yield more robust evaluation results. Each site would represent an independent and unique opportunity to see the concept in action. On the other hand, with different stakeholders and administrators involved, uniform program implementation is unlikely. Different service centers are likely to respond to different requests in different ways, depending on the nature of resources available to them. There definitely will be program-by-site interaction. Other problem areas that may be attributed to the multisite nature of the network include potential lack of standardization in data collection, organization, analysis, and verification. On the positive side, having multiple sites creates a sense of ownership of each center by its stakeholders. The site-specific nature of so many projects using the same "treatment" seriously limits the generalizability of the results if external validity is of major concern.

In an effort to meet individual school, student, and "community" needs, great latitude is allowed in the selection of the nature and duration of specific learn and serve activities. The end result often is heterogeneous and idiosyncratic treatments. A general service activity may be common to a school or group of schools—e.g., conservation and environmental protection, but have different experiences—e.g., water purity testing or recycling. Each of these experiences in turn might have a different academic link—e.g., science, social studies. Aggregating data to document overall program impact in such cases can be a data collection nightmare.

Just as different treatments may be in force, so might the degree and extent to which the treatment is being implemented in the same or different sites. Several different teachers in the same school and at the same grade levels may exhibit varying degrees of commitment to the "project"—e.g., recycling, resulting in a continuum of applications. Again, uniform data collection is inhibited, and meaningful documentation difficult. Budget constraints can always inhibit both implementation of projects and evaluation efforts.

A final implementation problem that has implications for instrumentation and data collection is the focus unit of the treatment. In some cases emphasis is on an individual student—e.g., gain in reading scores for the recipient of tutoring, in other cases the focus is on a larger group such as a class.

Sources of Threats to Internal Validity in Service-Learning Project Evaluations

Many factors contribute to evaluation challenges. Among these are limited evaluation and implementation budgets; lack of resources and planning, expertise, and experience; and the very nature of the uniqueness and complexity of the service-learning experience itself. There is also a tendency to focus on program protection rather than program improvement. Although the threats to internal and external validity are well documented (Campbell & Stanley, 1966), appreciation of them in the context of service-learning evaluation has not been addressed in the methodological literature.

External validity (generalizability of results) of service-learning evaluation projects is generally not of paramount concern. We are less concerned with generalizability questions than with those focused on making sure that **internal validity** is maintained—i.e., what was done in the name of service-learning was the thing that made the difference.

Table 7.1 contains some illustrations of factors that have been shown to contaminate internal validity. These are examples taken over the last several years from observations of state-

Table 7.1   Examples of Types and Sources of Internal Invalidity in Service-Learning Evaluations

Type	Example
History	The ripple effect on the nation of the April 1997 Summit on Volunteerism held in Philadelphia.
Maturation	Increases in math problem-solving skills of project class are attributed to homeless shelter construction project rather than developmental math instruction they were exposed to as a group in another class.
Instrumentation	Different readers used to assess degree of "altruism" on open-ended instrument that had not been pilot tested and validated in before and after design.
Statistical Regression	Students are selected to participate in a service project at a local nursing home on the basis of their high scores on a social responsibility scale. End of project scores show decline.
Selection	Students selected to participate in service-learning project are volunteers who have expressed high social service drive. Their altruism scores are also found to be high. Contrast data are collected from a convenience sample.
Mortality	After experiencing the frustration of tutoring younger students, those who are less motivated drop out of the project.
Testing	Reactivity/sensitivity of the pretesting with the "Value of Community Service" questionnaire administered to students engaged in beautification project around city buildings. When retested at conclusion of project, 86 percent of scores show increases.
Compensatory Rivalry/ Resentful Demoralization	Within-school students in contrast condition were not invited to participate in service rally at beginning of project year, or in "periodic" celebrations.

wide competitively funded individual projects. Some of these factors are more important than others. **Mortality**, for example, can be an important if sometimes uncontrollable factor. Unless the service activity is nonvoluntary—e.g., required through a course—lack of motivation to participate and see a project through to conclusion might be an important contributor to the failure to find implementation of the service experience. **Selection** is another potential source of data contamination. In particular, where self-selection of participants for inclusion or exclusion in service programs affects the composition of the target population, either participants or contrast groups can be distorted. As is so often the case, one of the most challenging problems in conducting service-learning evaluations is **instrumentation**.

Although most evaluators are accustomed to having to create or at least adapt existing instrumentation, this is almost always the case in service-learning projects. This is due in large part to the implementation problems described previously. A great deal of effort and time is therefore needed to produce valid and reliable assessments. Usually the kinds of outcome variables addressed in service-learning do not lend themselves to "standardized" measurement. A high school class, for example, adopts a local nursing home. One of the expected outcomes of the experience is an enhanced appreciation for the value of aged populations and the job of caregiving. Measurement of these variables would require a tailor-made device. The assessment of school and classroom learning outcomes always represents measurement challenges. Educational measurement and the resultant interpretations become even more complex when they must be linked to specific service experiences. The use of writing tasks (i.e., essays about service topics and activities) has been found to be an extremely valuable technique in this regard (Neal, Shumer, & Gorak, 1994). Scores from norm-referenced batteries are less than optimally relevant to the academic achievement links in most programs. Most instrumentation should be custom-made or at least adapted from existing measures.

Basis for Interpreting Evaluation Results

All evaluation involves some comparison. The statistical measurement yardstick might be an **absolute** value—e.g., 70 percent of the students will judge their service experience as Outstanding or Very Good, or **relative**—e.g., students having a service-learning experience will outperform non-service-learning students on a measure of science process skills. Most absolute standards are either self-evident (e.g., how close to 100 percent agreement they got) or are the result of some group standard setting where average judgments might be used (e.g., the mean estimated percent agreement was 62.). Standards are obviously involved in the two key elements of an evaluation design: the evaluation question (refer back to discussion of formatting in chapter 3), and the framework for data collection. A good evaluation question tells us what standard will be used, and the design tells us how we are going to gather the data to answer the question.

Figure 7.1 depicts six different sources of contrast or benchmark data. These sources are all **relative** since they represent groups or collections of data from which comparison data could be derived. Each source is then described, highlighting its advantages and disadvantages.

Figure 7.1 Alternative Sources of Benchmark Data for Interpretation of Evaluation Results

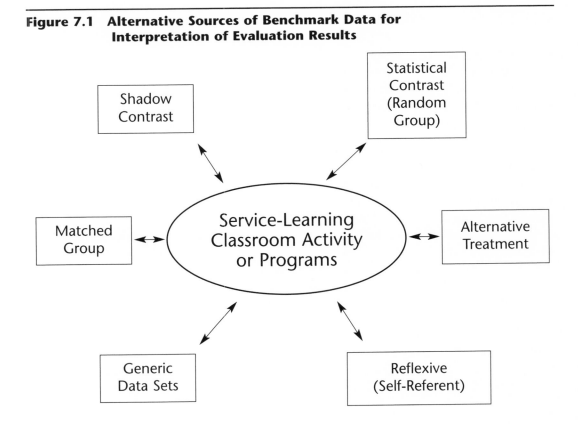

Four of the methods to be discussed require data to be gathered from actual groups or individual students (Statistical, Matched, Reflexive, and Alternative Treatment). One uses benchmark data that already exist (Generic) or requires data to be created (Shadow). For elaboration of the ideas presented here, see Rossi and Freeman (1993). The collection and analysis of these data can be accomplished in a quantitative, qualitative, or mixed-method design.

Statistical Contrast

The traditional approach to gathering comparison data is from a random sample of subjects like those treated in the program. Randomization as used here refers to the process of selecting or assigning whatever the sampling unit and ultimate analysis unit (e.g., individual student, teacher, classroom, school) to a condition (e.g., competing treatments, a treatment, and a contrast) so that each unit has an equally likely chance of being in each of the conditions.

Chance determines placement. Tables of random numbers or computer programs can be used effectively to accomplish randomization. Although less efficient and perhaps not useful with extremely large data sets, such manual methods as flipping coins, rolling dice, or drawing numbers from a hat can be used. An approximation of random selection can be accomplished by randomly entering a list of names or identification numbers and then taking every *n*th name as needed. The intent is to "equate" groups so that everyone begins on the same footing, and so that any factors that might influence the outcome measures, independent of the treatment, are controlled or at least confounded (i.e., don't have a systematic effect). Doing project evaluations in the real world usually does not allow for the luxury of employing complete randomization. It is impractical in public school settings, although it might be approximated by using, for example, classes that might not be using a particular service-learning activity at all or perhaps a different activity altogether. Sometimes groups can be found after the fact.

Alternative Treatment

Sometimes one is interested not just in whether an activity or a program was effective in an absolute sense, but in whether it was as good as or better than another approach. For example, the question might be asked: Is cross-age tutoring a better enhancer of the tutor's language arts skills than a more traditional drill and practice approach delivered via computer? When making these kinds of comparisons it is important to describe in great detail the exact nature of the "treatments" and their similarities and differences not just in terms of the specific activities and experiences, but also duration. It may be the case that two programs, projects, methods, activities, experiences, or what have you turn out to be "equally effective," but one costs twice as much as the other. In that case, the decision is made easier.

Reflexive Contrasts

Although frequently used, the "reflexive" or **pre-post** design is not very good. Sometimes it's all you can do, but the data-although interesting-do not allow us to say with any assurance exactly what happened. The philosophy of "I am my own control" makes intuitive sense, but changes like those observed with the treated or engaged students could have occurred naturally as a matter of course in school or developmentally. Sometimes this approach to setting a foundation for interpretation can be expanded to include multiple pre-assessments and multiple postassessments yielding what is sometimes called an **interrupted** time-series design.

Sometimes it is possible to identify an acceptable control or contrast group. When sensitive treatments are involved (e.g., attitudes toward senior citizens) pretesting, however, may generate a so-called pre-test effect that reacts with the dependent measure. To accommodate these difficulties, Campbell and Stanley (1966) have suggested the use of **retrospective pretesting**. Such a procedure allows the treated group to act as its own control, a particularly useful approach when self-report-dependent measures are involved. An allied problem is the phenomenon of "response-shift bias." Assume for a moment that you are going to be a participant in a workshop on problem-solving skills. The pretest contains an item such as the following: "I am a good problem solver." You strongly agree with the statement and so respond. After getting into the workshop, you find that you really aren't a very effective problem solver. At the end of a successful intervention, you are confident about the skills you have developed and again, but for a different reason, strongly agree with the statement, " I am a good problem solver." Obviously, a "no-difference" conclusion would be reached when evaluating the workshop. One method of "finding" some relevant contrast data involves, as the name of the method suggests, actually gathering pre-test data after the fact. One could, for example, have the workshop participant fill out an end-of-workshop questionnaire, providing a summative evaluation of its effects and values. The participant would then be asked to respond to the questionnaire as he or she would have if he or she had taken it prior to the experience. (Often it is not physically or operationally possible to gather real pre-test data.) Sometimes both administrations (the "true post" and the "retrospective pre") are combined into a single instrument. An example is presented in figure 7.2. Here the responses contain the contrasts desired. There is the added advantage that everyone is using the same bases for comparison called for in the responses. Obviously items needed to be added to this example to flesh out a more comprehensive instrument.

Generic Data Sets

Collections of data sets available from state and national sources can be useful benchmarks. Test norms available from publishers, for example, might provide a crude indication of academic achievement before and after a service-learning experience. Make no mistake, however; it is extremely difficult to get any substantial changes in standardized test scores. Census data and state summary statistics are also valuable. Sharing of data sets within the educational community in this regard should be encouraged.

Matched Groups

Although not held in the highest regard by all evaluators, the use of matching procedures can provide meaningful contrast data useful in evaluating programs, projects, and activities. The main advantage is that the evaluator has control over variables that may be (or that have been demonstrated in research to be) influential in affecting the effectiveness of the service-learning activity. An argument against matching is that for every variable on which individuals are matched there may be many others of equal or greater importance. It is unlikely that using this procedure will yield equivalent groups, but at least **comparable** groups can be identified. Variables that have been found in practice to be useful for matching purposes are percent of pupils on free or reduced lunch, average daily attendance, age, gender, per pupil expenditure, scores on a variety of standardized tests (especially ability and achievement), pupil/teacher ratios, and credentializing or certification data.

Shadow Contrast

When student or teacher data are not available for contrast purposes, sometimes they can be created. This is usually done with expert judgments. A general question like, "What would the ideal student look like on the _____ instrument?" might be asked. A group of experts would then fill out a form, and this "standard" profile would be used as a benchmark.

Students as Evaluators

A variety of data sources should be tapped when conducting a service-learning evaluation. The obvious ones have been mentioned already: teachers, community members, service targets, parents and school administrators, and, of course, students. Of these, students probably are the most important. They experience growth in two dimensions from the service-learning experience. The first of these is intellectual growth as academic skills and knowledge are acquired.

Figure 7.2   Sample Retrospective Response Document

School _____   Age _____

Date _____   Grade _____

Feelings about My School

This is not a test: Your teacher will read questions to you to find out how you think school went this year compared with last year. If there is no difference between this year and last year, it was about the SAME. Think before you answer and tell how you really feel. Draw a circle around your answer.

FOR EXAMPLE
    Students like to draw   (More   More   SAME
                              THIS)   LAST
                              year   year

This student thought that students like to draw more THIS year than LAST year.

1. Students like coming to school.	More THIS year	More LAST year	SAME
2. Students get into trouble in the hallways.	More THIS year	More LAST year	SAME
3. Our teachers help with schoolwork.	More THIS year	More LAST year	SAME
4. Parents helps with homework.	More THIS year	More LAST year	SAME
5. Students like to learn how to write.	More THIS year	More LAST year	SAME

As a result of the service experience itself, there also should be enhanced feelings about "citizenship" and the development of altruism. Being prime participants in and targets of the service-learning experience provides students a tremendous opportunity to serve as evaluators. Looking back to figure 2.2 for perspective, we could add an evaluator dimension and get something like the following:

	Participant	
	Student	Other
Evaluator Student		
Other		

We can see that the student evaluating him or herself and the student evaluating other participants theoretically could lead to 50 percent of the needed evaluation data. The idea of student self-evaluation, particularly of academic progress, is not new; we have been encouraging it in the classroom for a long time. With the rediscovery of portfolio assessment, the role of student in self-evaluation becomes even more important. There is obviously an empowering aspect of involving students in the evaluation process (Fetterman, 1998). Their ownership is significantly enhanced if they are part of the evaluation mechanism. Students can examine writing samples and respond to questions about why particular topics were chosen, what they learned from the writing experience, the best and worst features of what they produced recently compared to earlier efforts. The key here is student involvement in the process.

Students evaluating others, be they other students, participants, targets, or the experience itself, provides another opportunity to collect relevant information. There are good academic and psychological reasons for students to be involved in the evaluation process. What better illustration of the "scientific method" than to systematically work through an evaluation? The data generated can be used for a variety of problem-solving, calculation, and graphing tasks. The sense of ownership of the project is enhanced. Even the most quiet and reserved student can be motivated to form and express opinions. Young people will take leadership if given the opportunity, trust, and authority. It is also evident to anyone who has worked in the public schools for any period of time that kids can be incredibly creative.

Campbell, Edgar, and Halsted (1994) suggest some steps in designing a student-led evaluation:

- Secure school/project administration approval.
- Appoint a small diverse student steering committee.
- Review the evaluation process, paying particular attention to ethics and confidentiality.
- Let students decide what and how data are to be collected.
- Discuss questions of social desirability and validity.
- Let students analyze and report data.
- Request recommendations from students on the basis of results.

One hopes an example will illuminate the process.

A moderate-size inner-city middle school in rural Georgia had implemented two service-learning projects. One dealt with safety (water, gun, and bike). The other was a school-wide recycling effort. A play, *Cinderella and the Prince of Pollution*, was written and presented to elementary students in surrounding schools as an added attraction to the environmental effort. Students were involved in evaluating one aspect of the safety program by developing an observation checklist. Teams of students went to the parking lots periodically before school at the beginning of the project and again at the end of the school year to observe and record and helmet use. Recycling tonnage was calculated (approximately 4.4 tons per year) by source and grade and was graphed. Math problems were created from the data. And, finally, students created a survey form for parents to assess their participation in recycling efforts before and after the service project.

Doing an evaluation is a learning experience for anyone, but when the evaluator is also a participant, it can maximize the relevance of the data and the service-learning experience itself.

Planning Data Collection Designs

Three general categories of data collection designs exist, only one of which is considered here. They are: (1) experimental, (2) quasi-experimental, and (3) nonexperimental. Experimental designs are not considered because they have limited practical value for the informal kinds of in school service-learning evaluations considered in this volume. Nonexperimental designs do not yield credible results. We are left with quasi-experimental designs, which represent reasonable control of threats to design validity discussed previously in this chapter (see table 7.1).

It is often helpful to formalize a somewhat complex process such as data collection into a conceptual paradigm flow chart or other schematic. The convention will be used here where observation (O) with the same subscript means the same or equivalent measurement or observation no matter when it is taken or made. The schematic for our recommended design is as follows:

Service-Learning Group $\quad$ O_1 $\quad$ X_1 $\quad$ O_1

Contrast Group $\quad\quad\quad\quad$ (O_1) $\quad$ X $\quad$ (O_1)

Where:

$\quad$ O_1 $\quad=\quad$ an observation or measurement

$\quad$ X_1 $\quad=\quad$ service-learning experience or program

$\quad$ X $\quad=\quad$ traditional or alternative treatment

It has been mentioned several times throughout this book that the major role evaluation can play is in the **improvement** of a program or activity. This assumes that data are gathered frequently and examined with regard to (a) adequacy/fidelity of implementation, and (b) developing impact. Multiple observations will be needed to get the requisite data. We might better diagram our data collection plan as follows:

Service-Learning Group $\quad$ O_1 $\quad$ X_1 $\quad$ $\{O_k,\ O_k,\ O_k...\ O_k\}$ $\quad$ O_1

Contrast Group $\quad\quad\quad\quad$ O_1 $\quad$ X $\quad$ $\{O_k,\ O_k,\ O_k...\ O_k\}$ $\quad$ O_1

Where the O_k could be any repeated relevant observation.

The dotted horizontal line indicates that the groups were not constituted randomly. We have pre and post measures for both the service-learning group O_1 and the contrast group (O_1). The contrast data could come from any of six sources as noted in figure 7.1. Most likely it comes from a Matched or Alternative Treatment group. If only Shadow or Generic data are available, the configuration might look like this:

Service-Learning Group $\quad$ O_1 $\quad$ X_1 $\quad$ O_1

Contrast Group/Data $\quad\quad\quad\quad\quad\quad\quad\quad$ (O_1)

This assumes that exactly the same kinds of data are represented in the observations. Interpretation rests on the analysis of (a) the pre/post differences for the service-learning group, (b) the post differences between the service-learning and contrast data sets, or (c) the pre/post differences between the service-learning and contrast groups.

Recording and Analyzing Responses

Whatever method is used to collect the data-self-report, observation, or interview—there must be a convenient and efficient method of recording it for purposes of retrieval, manipulation, examination, or analysis. Since we are generally faced with relatively small sample sizes in service-learning projects, manual recording is probably sufficient. Most of our informal analyses will focus on frequency counts, percents, and means and standard deviations, so data entry by hand is probably not a big problem. If there are a large number of subjects and more complex analyses are anticipated, especially statistical ones, then use of any number of statistical packages available for personal computers is required (e.g., *Statistical Analysis Systems or Statistical Package for the Social Sciences*). Data can be entered by keystroke or with standard Scantron or National Computer System optical scan forms.

Although outside the intent of this book, there exist powerful statistical techniques useful in analyzing data from what was referred to earlier as nonequivalent contrast design. One such technique is analysis of covariance (ANCOVA). This procedure allows "post" scores to be statistically adjusted for initial differences between treatment and contrast groups. This technique, usually using the "pre" measure as the adjuster, provides for greater power and precision in the analyses.

One final statistical comment relates to the analyses of simple differences between post experience averages (means) for experimental and contrast groups. Sophisticated procedures can be used to analyze these differences, but they can be influenced significantly by having large groups. One straightforward approach to the interpretation of the meaning of those mean differences is through the examination of **effect size**.

Effect Size = Mean Treated Group **minus** Mean of the Contrast Group **divided** by the standard deviation of the contrast group.

Symbolically:

$$ES = \frac{M_T - M_C}{S_C}$$

If this index comes out to have a value somewhere around +.30, results are generally interpreted as being meaningful and perhaps educationally significant.

For comprehensive and comprehensible coverage of statistical topics, see Freed (1991) and Sprinthall (1994).

Data Collection Management

A useful administrative tool for evaluators and project directors is the data management plan (chart). It is a simple notion but one that allows the evaluator to see the entire evaluation design at a glance. The plan is a two-way chart listing the evaluation questions along the Y-axis and the evaluation events along the X-axis. Eight evaluation questions have been turned into the data management chart presented in figure 7.3. The project involved "at-risk" ninth-grade students who were to create books and audiotapes for students in the state Academy for the Blind. It was hoped that the sighted students, because of their involvement in the creative academic activity, would enhance their general language arts skills, in particular reading and writing. In addition, one would hope that such positive community involvement would have a positive effect on discipline, attendance, and attitude toward school.

Eight evaluation questions were derived from consideration of the major goals of the project. Will students participating in a service-learning experience:

Figure 7.3   Data Management Plan for Academy for the Blind High School Service-Learning Project

Evaluation Question	Data Source	Instrumentation	Data Point	Person(s) Responsible	Analysis Procedure
One (Service-Learning)	Service-Learning Students	Opinionnaire	Spring	Project Coordinator	t-test/Descriptive
Two (Reading)	Service-Learning Students	Reading Achievement Scores	Fall/Spring	Project Coordinator	t-test
Three (Writing)	Service-Learning Students	Writing Sample	Fall/Spring	Teachers	t-test
Four (Attitude—Reading)	Service-Learning Students	Attitude Scale	Spring	Project Coordinator	t-test
Five (Attitude—Writing)	Service-Learning Students	Attitude Scale	Spring	Project Coordinator	t-test
Six (Attitude—School)	All Students	Attitude Scale	Fall/Spring	Evaluator	t-test/Descriptive
Seven (Discipline)	All Students	Archival Data	Fall/Spring	Project Coordinator	Descriptive
Eight (Service-Learning)	Academy for	Questionnaire	Spring	Evaluator	Descriptive

EQ₁: Positively evaluate their experiences?

EQ₂: Increase their reading achievement?

EQ₃: Improve their writing competency?

EQ₄: Enhance their attitude toward reading activities?

EQ₅: Enhance their attitude toward writing activities?

EQ₆: Enhance their general attitude toward school?

EQ₇: Show a decrease in discipline referrals?

And with regard to students from the Georgia Academy for the Blind, will they

EQ₈: Positively evaluate their participation in a service-learning experience?

Two of the most important categories of our data management chart are Data Source and Persons Responsible. These two components are particularly critical in data collection and should help the evaluator do a better job of planning for a variety of activities, such as the creation or ordering of instrumentation, assigning specific responsibility for gathering information and data entry, and scheduling data collection times and locations. Another way in which a chart similar to that in figure 7.3 can be helpful is with regard to creating reports. The chart captures the entire evaluation event and should allow the evaluator to create a more comprehensive and effective communication of the results.

The sum total of the problems discussed in this chapter obviously leads to the conclusion that an eclectic approach to designing service-learning evaluations is necessary. Forcing service-learning evaluation into traditional X and O configurations doesn't make sense; neither does relying exclusively on costly qualitative methods. A variety of methods (mixed methods) to meet a variety of needs seems to be a reasonable guideline. This is surely not an earthshaking insight, but when it happens to your evaluation psyche, it can be a true revelation. Case study methodology and aggregated multiple case studies in addition perhaps to goal-free and responsive approaches have been used profitably to evaluate service-learning projects. But new approaches are always needed. It is hoped that this brief vignette will provoke an exchange of ideas and methods. Don't forget to contact the National Service-Learning Cooperative at the University of Minnesota for ideas and help on evaluating service-learning activities and programs (e-mail: serve@tc.umn.edul; Website: http://www.nicsl.coled.umn.edu). The exciting aspect of doing evaluations is finding a methodology that helps meet a important data-need challenges, and the evaluation of service-learning projects surely poses many challenges.

Referenceography

Campbell, D. T., & Stanley, J. C. (1966). *Experimental and quasi-experimental designs for research*. Chicago: Rand McNally.

Campbell, P., Edgar, S., & Halsted, A. (1994). Students as evaluators: A model for program evaluation. *Phi Delta Kappan*, 76(2), 160–165.

Cook, T. D., & Campbell, D. T. (1979). *Quasi-experimentation: Design and analysis issues for field settings*. Chicago: Rand McNally.

Fetterman, D. M. (1998). *Empowerment evaluation*. Newbury Park, CA: Sage.

Freed, M. N. (1991). *Handbook of statistical procedures and their computer applications to education and the behavioral sciences*. New York: American Council on Education/Macmillan.

Merriam, S. B. (1988). *Case study research in education (A qualitative approach)*. (Second Edition). San Francisco: Jossey-Bass.

Mohr, L. B. (1992). *Impact analysis for program evaluation*. Newbury Park, CA: Sage.

Neal, M., Shumer, R., & Gorak, K. S. (1994). *Evaluation: The key to improving service-learning programs*. Minneapolis: Center for Experiential Education and Service-Learning, University of Minnesota.

Popham, W. J. (1993). *Educational evaluation* (Third Edition). Boston: Allyn & Bacon.

Reichardt, C. S., & Rallis, S. F. (1994). *The qualitative-quantitative debate: New perspectives*. San Francisco: Jossey-Bass.

Rossi, P. H., & Freeman, H. E. (1993). *Evaluation-A systematic approach*. (Fifth Edition). Newbury Park, CA: Sage.

Serow, R. C. (1997). Research and evaluation on service-learning: The case for holistic assessment. In A. A. Waterman (Ed.) *Service-learning: Applications from the research*. Mahwah, NJ: Erlbaum, 13–24.

Shumer, R. (1994). Community-based learning: Humanizing education. *Journal of Adolescence*, 17(August), 357–367.

Sprinthall, R. C. (1994). *Basic statistical analysis*. Boston: Allyn & Bacon.

Waterman, A. S. (1997). *Service-learning: Applications from the research*. Mahwah, NJ: Lawrence Erlbaum.

Case Study

The evaluation of Adopt-a-Senior was a low-budget effort. A total of $1,500 was available for everything—duplication of instruments, travel, data collection, data entry and analysis, report preparation, and all the evaluator's visits to the site.

One of the data collection problems to be addressed was the fact that different grade level students were having the "service experience" at different times of the year.

Given that prekindergartners are struggling just to adjust to the school climate and that kindergartners are totally focused on "readiness" for the regular school program, impact data was gathered from first and second graders only.

Although no primary school could be identified in the immediate area from which to gather benchmark data, contrast data were available from first- and second-grade classes in a matched-school in a neighboring county. Variables used to match were (a) percent of students on free and reduced lunch and breakfast, (b) average daily attendance, (c) per pupil expenditure, and (d) average total battery scores on the *Iowa Tests of Basic Skills*.

THOUGHT QUESTION
Given the five evaluation questions and the foregoing information on the contrast school, how would you conduct the data collection?

Following was the nonequivalent contrast design for the evaluation.

Adopt-a-Senior Classes	O_1	O_2	O_3	X_{SL}	O_1	O_2	O_3	O_4	O_5
Contrast Classes	O_1	O_2	O_3	X_C	O_1	O_2	O_3	O_4	O_5

Where:

X_{SL} = curriculum with service-learning infusion

X_C = standard curriculum for contrast classes

0_1 = Ideas about Young People and Older People measure

0_2 = Attitude toward Reading

0_3 = reading performance measure

0_4 = student evaluations of their service-learning experience

0_5 = Pine Tree Manor residents' evaluations of their intergenerational experience

To facilitate collection of the evaluation data for all concerned, a "management chart" like the one portrayed in figure 7.3 was developed. It is presented in the following figure 7.4. A couple of comments are in order. First, the statistical test of choice should have been a somewhat sophisticated analysis called analysis of covariance. This procedure allows for examination of the statistical significance of the differences in the spring scores on the attitudes toward elderly and reading attitude measures for the Adopt-a-Senior and Contrast students, adjusting for the Spring scores. You must be able to match the fall and spring scores by name to do this analysis. However, another real-world problem presented itself. Unfortunately data were collected anonymously so only a *t*-test was possible. This was done without to the evaluator's knowledge, again stressing the importance of communication during the entire evaluation process. Second, as an attempt to triangulate some data, a sample of the Pine Tree Manor residents were asked to fill out the "Ideas about Young People and Older People" instrument *as they thought the young children would fill it out*. It was hoped that the data from the two sources would converge to give a credible picture of the impact of the program.

Figure 7.4 Data Management Plan, Adopt-a-Senior Service-Learning Program

Evaluation Question	Data Source	Instrumentation	Data Point	Person(s) Responsible	Analysis Procedure
One (Attitude toward Elderly)	Students (Target & Contrast)	New 18-item attitude scale	Fall/Spring	Project Coordinator	Descriptive/ Statistical Test
Two (Reading Attitude)	Students (Target & Contrast)	Reading Attitude Scale	Fall/Spring	Project Coordinator	Descriptive/ Statistical Test
Three (Reading Achievement)	Students (& Technical Manual)		Fall/Spring	Project Coordinator	Descriptive/ Statistical Test
Four (Service-Learning: Student)	Students	Questionnaire	Spring	Evaluator	Descriptive
Five (Service-Learning: Resident)	Residents	Interview Form, Student Attitude Survey from EQ_1	Spring	Evaluator	Descriptive

Eight

Reporting and Using Answers

No matter the nature of the activity, whether individual or group, it's human nature to want to know how one did. In addition, we are usually interested in what others think about our performance. Those engaged in service-learning have this same desire to know. All the stakeholders are entitled to a report of how things went. Some might be interested in quantitative things, such as how many thousands of pounds of newspaper got recycled or students scored on tests. Others might be more concerned with qualitative things, such as the attitudes of participants toward the service activity or opinions of partners about the value of the project and how it could be improved.

Throughout the evaluation process, efforts should be made to help ensure that the results can be used to help make decisions or simply to obtain a better understanding of the success of the program or project. In the latter sense of the word, **use** is intended to mean **illuminate** the program to help see relationships, processes, and outcomes. What we don't want to happen is to have evaluation studies conducted simply to fulfill a requirement or to be completed for public relations reasons. The "symbolic" use of evaluation is a sham and marks anyone knowingly involved (decision makers or evaluator) as unethical. There is a sense in which a non-decision-oriented use of evaluation data make sense, and that is to persuade an audience of the value of the program. This assumes no intent to deceive. The evaluation should cause us to pause and **reflect**.

How do we ensure that the evaluation results will be used and in an appropriate way? There is nothing the evaluator can do to guarantee legitimate use of the results, but it is hoped that best professional practice has been followed throughout the evaluation design and implementation process so that the likelihood of appropriate use of the results has been increased. Staying in touch with the stakeholders is not only smart politically, but it also assists in laying the foundation for maximizing use of the results. Touching base with those stakeholders periodically helps keep the projects moving. Newsletters can be very helpful in this regard. *Involving the stakeholders at every stage* should be among the most important tenets in the evaluator's philosophy. Nowhere is that tenet more significant than when it comes time to communicate the results of the evaluation.

With this orientation in mind, what are some general guidelines for report preparation?

General Guidelines for Report Preparation

Following are some commonsense things that an evaluator or project director can do that might help in the communication process.

1. *Prepare relevant audiences and, where appropriate, the public and press for the impending report.* A preliminary written statement or briefing session focused on the aims, interests, and expected outcomes should be provided. Not only does this aid communication, but the potential public relations value cannot be underestimated.
2. *Prepare an executive and tabular summary and synopsis of the study results for general release.* Breakdowns accompanied by description of samples, treatments, and factors known or hypothesized to have influenced the results will help convey a clear picture of the conclusions. Share them with all stakeholders.
3. *Emphasize contingency variables in communicating results.* Cost factors, construction/renovation disturbances, a partner pulling out, our lack of participation might mar success of

service-learning programs. The presence of competing innovative approaches and programs in the school should also be considered.

4. *Prepare an overall summary of the results.* It is better for the local educational agency to prepare the summary than to allow those less informed about the program and evaluation procedures to make possibly erroneous interpretations or draw unwarranted conclusions. Emphasis should be placed on the broad significance of the results, particularly as they relate to improvement of the teaching-learning process and community outreach.

Specific Guidelines for Report Preparation

In addition to the foregoing general suggestions, research and experience have suggested some specific reporting procedures that might substantially help influence decision makers. Among these are suggestions with regard to:

Focus

- Involve stakeholders (and other relevant audiences) in outlining the purposes and format of the report. They also need to sign off on the content and interpretation of the results.
- Write custom-made reports for specific audiences where possible.
- Prepare a mock or simulated report for early discussion.
- Solicit interpretations of results from stakeholders.
- Link presentation of results to major objectives, issues, and decisions.
- Be sensitive to clients' and stakeholders' identities, feelings, and interests.

Structure/format

- Begin with a nontechnical executive summary.
- Use as many words as necessary but as few as possible.
- Use nontechnical terminology and interesting language.
- Use illustrations, examples, graphs, charts, pictures, and figures.
- Detail strengths and weaknesses (limitations) of the evaluation.
- Describe evaluation plan and procedures in as much detail as possible. (This will depend on sophistication of audience.)
- Include recommendations for use of results.
- If judgments were made describe criteria used.
- Put highly technical information in appendices or a separate report so that unsophisticated readers won't be intimidated by this information.

Presentation

- Pay attention to visual appeal and organization.
- Use multimedia where possible (e.g., slides, videotape).
- Use professionally designed and colorful graphics if possible.

Timing

- Make periodic formal and informal reports.
- Ensure that reports are delivered when appropriate and on time to relevant audiences.
- Meet personally with decision makers frequently.

It's time to outline the report. Be sure to check the outline with stakeholders, staff, and relevant audiences.

Suggested Learn and Serve Evaluation Plan/Report Format

Much of this outline can be used for *both* the plan of the evaluation and a report of its results.

Executive Summary

Summary of design (e.g., sample, instrumentation, collection points) and specific major findings of interest to project director, funding agency, or potential adopter. (No *more* than one single-spaced page).

Background/Overview

Brief synopsis of general thrust/intent of project. Provide reader with sense of need for service-learning project. Summarize general purpose(s) and include an overview of major activities.

Project Goals

One objective might be created for each of the following categories: Academic Achievement, Attitudes, and Civics (broadly conceived to include appreciation of the concept and behaviors associated with service, helping your fellow man, character, and being a responsible citizen in and out of school—for example,

- to increase student reading comprehension by engaging in a cross-age tutoring experience;
- to improve student attitudes toward senior citizens by working on joint projects at a nursing facility; and
- to enhance the appreciation of the importance of community service by conducting school-wide recycling efforts

Overview of Treatment

How were goals addressed? A chart outlining goal(s) by treatment(s) by target(s) helps readers see the "big picture."

Evaluation Objectives

Major dependent variables (i.e., achievement, attitude, civics) need to be translated into operational definitions of expected project outcomes for targets (usually students)—for example,

- Will involvement in a school-wide recycling program increase scores on an environmental issues awareness scale?
- Will students engaged in weekly reading tutoring sessions increase their vocabularies more than peer students not engaged in such activities?
- Will students receiving tutoring increase their scores on the Woodcock Reading Mastery Tests?

Description of Targets

Sample sizes, selection procedures, and types of targets are described, together with appropriate demographic data if relevant. Obviously student data are important, but additional elaboration of other participants might be necessary to view total impact of project (e.g., teachers, administrators, and community groups/members, particularly partners and clients served).

Instrumentation

All data collection methods are described with references and/or technical data. Both quantitative and qualitative methods are encouraged.

Data Collection/Management

Here a chart helps the audience see what data will be gathered, when, from whom, and by whom. Data analysis procedures might be described here, particularly if they are unusual or elaborate—e.g., content analysis or rubric creation and scoring. Avoid technical discussions or overly sophisticated methodologies. Statistical overkill can lead to a failure to communicate and rejection of findings. This is a critical section as most Learn and Serve projects take place in multiple sites.

Limitations

Were there events during implementation of the project or conduct of the evaluation that would bias the results and their interpretation? Be sensitive to public relations issues, but remember that too much candor can be harmful.

Results

Major findings organized by evaluation question are presented. Evaluative interpretations are presented. What conclusions are warranted? Use graphics where relevant. Simple bar graphs or pie charts help make the data interesting. Avoid the use of jargon, use correct, uncomplicated, and interesting language. Don't overlook summaries of interviews and anecdotal information. Direct quotes from participants and targets help to make the report a real-life document.

Recommendations

One of the reasons why communicating evaluation results is so important is that service-learning projects are pledged to perpetuate themselves. What implications, results, and conclusions from this edition of the project are suggested for future versions?

What is described here is an idealized situation where there is probably an individual responsible for preparing an evaluation report. Some sort of feedback is required, but it might be more informal than that described. A parent newsletter at the end of the year can have a tremendous positive impact.

Data-Based Recommendations

Decisions about the fate and future of a program are of much greater variety than simple save it or scrap it pronouncements. One must realize that innovative programs will be saved if at all possible unless they are much too costly, are poorly received by participants, or are too intrusive into the ongoing school program. Realism must also be considered in wrestling with "political" aspects of decision making. Sometimes decision makers support or reject a project simply because it does or does not make the school look good. The likelihood is that unless there are major flaws or funding problems the service-learning will continue. But continue in what form? The evaluator can help significantly in the recommendation department.

There are two major controversial questions with which evaluators are frequently faced: (1) Should the evaluator in fact make a value judgment about the program/project? and (2) Should the evaluator make recommendations about the program/project? Yes to both questions. The evaluator is more than a collector and processor of information. Because of their very intimate association with both the program/project and the details of the evaluation, evaluators are probably in the best position to render an overall judgment of the worth of the program (and each of the subcomponents) and to suggest changes in the program. These changes may relate to content, process, or application of the results. They also may relate to adjustments in the evaluation design if the study is to be replicated. Whether recommendations are made part of the report should be negotiated by the evaluator and stakeholders (clients).

Some idea of the variety of recommendations that might be made on the basis of evaluation results is suggested by a list compiled by the National Association of Partners in Education (1996). The suggestions, some of which are listed below, include a great range of actions. Some might be as dramatic as terminating a program and/or reconstructing it from the ground up. Most recommendations, however, are aimed at fine-tuning and are incremental in nature. Evaluation should be an impetus to action. Informed decisions might be to:

- improve or refine an existing program,
- institutionalize or make permanent a current program,
- retarget participant groups,
- reassign participants or volunteers,
- redesign management,
- revisit expectations of the program's impact,
- assess the link between classroom and service activity,
- change indicators of program impact,
- examine school-community relations,
- focus greater effort on establishing parental involvement,
- reexamine implementation schedule,
- consolidate activities,
- motivate a cost-benefit analysis,
- motivate a cost-effectiveness analysis,
- expand time allotments to planning, implementing, reflection, and/or celebration activities, or
- seek out new and different partners.

Other ideas for recommendations should be stimulated by the list of kinds of decisions to be made and questions asked about service-learning projects and activities included in chapter 3.

Cost Considerations

The evaluator and the crew of data gatherers are concerned with two categories of costs. The first and most obvious relates to costs associated with the actual conduct of the service-learning evaluation. Mundane expenditures related to salaries and materials purchase are high on this list. The other category of cost consideration provides data for decision makers concerning the probable cost-effectiveness and benefits to be derived from implementing the program or project.

Costs Associated with Implementing the Evaluation

A commonly used rule of thumb is that the usual costs associated with the operation of an evaluation program are 10 percent of the total budget. The range may be from a low of 2 percent to a high of 20 percent or more, depending on the number and complexity of the evaluation questions, project duration, and the expense of data collection. Many factors contribute to bottom-line evaluation program implementation costs, among them:

Salaries. This can be a significant item if the project has substantial funding and is quite large in scope. To this category we must add benefits packages, which appear to increase with each change in national government.

Data Collection. A large item in most evaluation projects is the purchase, development, and/or duplication of instrumentation. One could also include the time to train data collectors and their time in the field as they actually administer instruments. Scoring and recording costs should also be estimated.

Travel/Per Diem. Costs for meetings and travel to data collection sites for full-time staff and data collectors as necessary. If the budget allows, presentations at state and national professional meetings are appropriate to learn of recent developments and share results of the home project.

Data Processing. With the advent of computers, data processing has become quite cost- effective. However, one must still wrestle with data entry. Optical scanning is probably most efficient, but keyboard entry by a whiz also can be efficient. Although quite easy to accomplish, data processing and analysis always takes longer than projected.

Printing/Duplicating. Don't forget to allow for the costs of report production, particularly if different reports are projected for multiple audiences. Some instrumentation may have to be copied and duplicated. This can be a big item if survey methods are used.

Office Supplies/Communication. Don't have fewer telephones than you need. You can never have too many writing pads and pens and the usual stationery, envelopes, stamps, mailers; the list is endless. Put computers and printers on your wish list.

Miscellaneous. This catchall category could include consultants and overhead expenses.

Planning, perhaps using *Program Evaluation and Review Techniques* (PERT) and GANTT (Clark, 1952) charts and volunteers can help reduce costs.

Evaluating Program Impact Costs

The assessment of the various cost dimensions of an implemented service-learning project are much more complex than the budget of the evaluation. At the outset we note that any costs of or funds spent for a program or project represent opportunities or benefits lost. The term **lost** as used here means **spent in lieu of**. In implementing a community environmental awareness and beautification project, a school has opted *not* to spend it for a technology project, hospital service, or on a homeless children's shelter education program. Spending represents a series of choices. Conscious (and, one hopes, rational) decisions have been made about costs. What cost-related data can decision makers use in assessing a program?

We are not talking about great amounts of money with most service-learning programs. There are many school partners, both public and private, more than willing to contribute staff time and organizational dollars to a school-community project. It's good for the community and business.

Popham (1993, p. 308) has summarized succinctly four cost-analysis procedures: cost-feasibility, cost-utility, cost-effectiveness, and cost-benefit. The first two types take place *before* implementation (or selection facilitation) and the second two, *after* the implementation.

Cost-feasibility simply considers the cost of implementing a single program or optional programs relative to available funds. We have all faced the problem of affordability, and school systems continually wrestle with budget constraints. If a repair and renovation project for the local homeless shelter is projected to be $10,125, and our service budget has only $7,350, the hammer-and-nail project may not be a realistic option. We might be able to scale down the project or find outside funds, but realistic fiscal parameters have to be established.

Cost-utility analysis involves estimates or judgments of the likelihood that each of two or more competing programs will yield outcomes that are useful and of value to the intended target groups. Judgments about utility of the programs are gathered in arbitrary units—for example, "On a scale from 1 to 10, how much will the [fill in the name of described service-learning project] contribute to the academic and civic education of our students?" Data are gathered and aggregated from a number of judges, including students, teachers, and other interested stakeholders. The gross cost (C) of the program is then divided by the mean Utility estimates (U). For example:

Project	Gross Cost (C)	Mean Utility (U)	Utility Index (C/U)
Homeless Shelter Repair	$10,125	5.9	$1,716.10
Intergenerational	$ 5,240	6.6	$ 793.94
Animal Shelter	$ 1,500	7.4	$ 208.33

Our cost-utility choice is the Animal Shelter project. It's also nice that this project has the lowest gross cost. If projects have similar utility indices, we select the one that costs less.

Examining **cost-effectiveness** requires the evaluator to document the effectiveness (in a criterion sense) of the program(s). The cost of the program is divided by some measure of effectiveness—e.g., increase in number of reading achievement items answered correctly. That result can be evaluated in an absolute sense, or several programs can be compared using a common measure. For example, we found that we got an average increase of 14.3 items answered correctly per dollar from this program. Is that acceptable? Ask the teachers and administrators. The answer is probably based on how valuable those items are perceived to be.

This leads us to the final cost-analysis method to be considered, **cost-benefit** assessment (sometimes referred to as benefit-cost analysis). The biggest obstacle to conducting a cost-benefit analysis is the conversion of outcome or benefits to dollar values. The comparison is program dollars to benefit dollars. Benefit dollars can be estimated (the usual procedure) or derived from monitoring over time. With regard to a reading program, for example, let's assume that there was a reasonable way to estimate the dollar value of being able to read better. It would be hypothesized that better readers (or writers or speakers or figurers) will make more money, are more likely to be promoted or to graduate, or get bigger and better scholarships. The following data might be realized from two program comparisons.

	Gross Cost	Benefit Value	Cost Benefit (C/B)	Net Benefit
McKenna Program	$18,725	$16,586	1.13	–$2,139
Grover Program	$13,830	$27,418	.50	$12,588

It doesn't take a rocket scientist to see that if benefits exceed costs, we have a winner. In this case, Grover is in first place.

Doing cost analyses is hard work. They often don't get done because they are not perceived as necessary once the feasibility criterion is met. Comprehensive evaluations look at *both* impact and cost.

Factors Related to Utilization of Evaluation Results

Two major factors influence the use of evaluation results. One is controllable by the evaluator. The basic evaluation itself—focus, design, implementation—will have credibility to the extent that the evaluator had followed sound professional practice. Reporting of the results also can be managed by the evaluator. There are, of course, many sociopolitical factors impinging on the evaluation environment that are outside the control of evaluators, stakeholders, and decision makers. The influence of both these factors can be seen in the list of problems inhibiting the use of evaluation results compiled by Cox (1977). His list includes:

- Mismatch in roles/styles of stakeholder and evaluator
- Lack of rigor in evaluation design

- Excess methodological rigor to the detriment of relevance of report
- Lack of utility in recommendations
- Lack of timeliness of report
- External influences (money, politics) having more importance than the data
- Failure to communicate results in a usable way

While the well-designed evaluation may be a thing of beauty, if the results are not used to (1) aid in decision making, (2) support previous decisions or actions, and (3) establish or change attitudes, then a valuable opportunity and time, effort, and resources are likely to be lost. Evaluation without utilization is like unrequited love: lots of expectations and anticipations, but no satisfaction or fulfillment.

There are probably three kinds of problem areas in evaluation utilization, each as bad as the others: underutilization, overutilization (particularly of poorly designed and implemented studies), and nonutilization. Depending on the context, each of these inappropriate practices can have devastating effects. Unscrupulous administrators have been known to use evaluation as a cat's paw to meet their own needs. A problem sometimes encountered is what might be called "compliance control evaluations," which are usually undertaken by superordinate organizations. Such evaluations are frequently conducted with little required collaborative effort from the staff of the project or program being evaluated. Evaluations are easy to critique. A clever administrator can "fuddle" away implementation or evaluation recommendations or can claim that the evaluation supports changes already implemented. Evaluation data, however, should be viewed in the same way as the data a driver gets from a speedometer, as an aid in making decisions about progress toward a goal or goals. Superficial or cosmetic utilization is a sham and unprofessional. If it's worth doing, it's worth doing right.

The consideration of utilization raises perhaps another valuable role that the evaluator might perform—that of change agent. In most situations, utilization of evaluation data results in incremental change rather than one or more dramatic changes. Evaluators should be more than simply providers of information. The evaluator is in a very opportunistic position (in the most positive sense of that phrase) to aid in the application of evaluation results. Through continuing and intimate contact with all segments of the local educational system and community, the evaluator can see and suggest ways to use the results.

The time to plan for the use of evaluation results is at the beginning of the program development process. The likelihood that the evaluation results will be used significantly increases if the information needs of the stakeholders are discussed and the most relevant questions are asked and answered. Common sense can do about as much as anything to help ensure that evaluation results will be used. A review of relevant research suggests conclusions that confirm what common sense would suggest—that the likelihood of having usable evaluation results is increased if:

1. Evaluations are appropriate in approach, methodological sophistication, and intensity.
2. The decisions to be made are perceived as significant to users and of a sort considered appropriate for the application of formally collected data.
3. Evaluation findings are consistent with the beliefs and expectations of the users.
4. Users consider the data reported in the evaluation to be credible and relevant to their problems.
5. A minimum amount of information from other sources conflicts with the results of the evaluation.

Sometimes common sense is obvious but worth reinforcing.

In the final analysis, utilization may be the key to an effective evaluation system. At times the key is rusty and stubborn, but if we are to unlock the door of truth we must make maximum effort toward utilization. The discovered truth may not set us free, but it should (1) make us feel better, and (2) make for more effective and efficient realization of human resources.

Well, strike up the band, turn on the searchlights, and light the fireworks—that long-awaited moment has arrived: decision-making time! Our efforts to design relevant questions, set standards, and create a framework for collecting and processing data will now be rewarded by having presented the opportunity to answer our most important evaluation questions.

Decision Making

Evaluations are undertaken to produce data which, it is hoped, will reduce uncertainty about effectiveness and efficiency. Data are gathered, sifted, and summarized. Decisions using those data must then be made. These are often complex and sometimes gut-wrenching decisions. There are probably as many theories about how to make evaluation decisions as there are decision makers. To illustrate elements in the decision-making process, the management metaphor delineated by Stufflebeam (1983) is employed.

Types of Decisions

Stufflebeam et al. (1971) suggest that managers, administrators, and coordinators may be called on to make any or all of four basic types of decisions. They are:

Planning:	The primary focus here is on what objectives should be sought. An evaluation of the acceptability of current objectives relative to needs may be undertaken. These are policy decisions, and data are needed to help establish or sustain goals. This corresponds to one of the initial steps in creating any service-learning activity or program, a survey of needs, school site, and community.
Structuring:	Given the objectives identified or confirmed at the planning level, what means are available to meet them? Resources and the advantages or disadvantages of alternative procedures in creating an action plan or design are considered. Both school and community resources are sought.
Implementing:	Once the objectives have been set and an action plan mounted, evaluation of the implementation must be undertaken. Concern is on how to refine the procedures. Formative evaluation procedures can be very helpful here, as the intent is to streamline the process.
Recycling:	The basic question here relates to goal attainment in a summative sense. Quality control of products or services is a continuing process. Is the end product worth the effort, and should it be continued?

Obviously the nature of the decision to be made will be dictated by the question to be answered. The reader is referred back to chapter 3 for a review of the kinds of questions that might be asked about service-learning activities and programs, and how phrasing of evaluation questions with criteria and standards built-in can dramatically facilitate decision making. Table 8.1 contains a summary of the four kinds of decision categories and sample evaluation questions.

It can be seen that with the right evaluation questions, decision making (and, to some extent, utilization considering Recycling questions) is completed almost automatically—again emphasizing the importance of asking the right questions.

The interpretation and communication of evaluation results—whether to students, colleagues, parents, or members of the community in general—requires careful preparation and a thorough understanding of evaluation methodology, what influences it, and how the results can be used. It is a very demanding and critical task.

Table 8.1 Sample Decision Categories and Evaluation Questions

Decision Category	Decision Question	Evaluation Question
Planning	What are the three most important community service needs as seen through the eyes of the city commission?	What are the three top ranked community needs derived from student interviews of city commission members?
Structuring	Which one of the three ways in which the community beautification projects identified by the city commission and students can best be linked to school involvement?	Which of the three academic links are preferred by teachers and students?
Implementing	Is the recycling program operating as intended?	Is at least 70 percent of the student body actively participating in the newspaper and phone book recycling program?
Recycling	Are students in classes participating in the environmental awareness/beautification service-learning program learning more basic science concepts than nonparticipating classes?	Are end-of-year science scores on the Science section of the *Stanford Achievement Test* (35 percent higher for participating than nonparticipating service-learning classes?

Referenceography

Alkin, M. C., & Solmon, L. C. (Eds.) (1983). *The costs of evaluation*. Beverly Hills, CA: Sage.

Clark, N. (1952). *The Gantt chart*. London: Pitman & Sons.

Cox, G. B. (1977). Managerial style: Implications for the utilization of program evaluation information. *Evaluation Quarterly*, 1(3), 499–508.

Morris, L. L., Taylor Fitz-Gibbon, C., & Freeman, M. E. (1987). *How to communicate evaluation findings*. Newbury Park, CA: Sage.

National Association of Partners in Education (1996). *Service-learning & business/education partnerships* (A guide for service-learning coordinators). Alexandria, VA: National Association of Partners in Education.

Patton, M. Q. (1997). *Utilization-focused evaluation*. (Third Edition). Newbury Park, CA: Sage.

Popham, W. J. (1993). *Educational evaluation*. (Third Edition). Boston: Allyn & Bacon.

Royse, D. (1992). *Program evaluation*. Chicago: Nelson-Hall. See chapter 9, "Writing the Evaluation Report."

Smith, N. L. (1982). *Communication strategies in evaluation.* Newbury Park, CA: Sage.

Stufflebeam, D. L. (1983). The CIPP model for program evaluation. In G. F. Madaus, M. Scriven, & D. L. Stufflebeam (Eds.). *Evaluation models (Viewpoints on educational and human service evaluation.* Boston: Kluwer-Nijhoff, 287–310.

Stufflebeam, D. L., Foley, W. J., Gephart, W. J., Guba, E. G., Hammond, R. L., Merriman, H. O., & Provus, M. W. (1971). *Educational evaluation and decision-making.* Itasca, IL: Peacock.

Thompson, M. S. (1980). *Benefit-cost analysis for program evaluation.* Beverly Hills, CA: Sage.

Wolcott, H. F. (1990). *Writing up qualitative research.* Newbury Park, CA: Sage.

Wolf, R. A. (1969). A model for curriculum evaluation. *Psychology in the Schools,* 6, 107–108.

Case Study

The reader's indulgence is requested with regard to the Final Report because most of the information—except for results—is redundant. An attempt has been made to make the Final Report as realistic as possible. The reader might also consider how stakeholders will be informed. For example, perhaps a nontechnical version of the Executive Summary could be shared with students and parents. In addition a version for media consumption might also be created. And, for heaven's sake, don't forget the partners, in this case the residents of Pine Manor.

> **THOUGHT QUESTION**
> Being a highly motivated reader, the author is sure that you want to use the data of the case studies in chapters 3–7 and the outline in this chapter to create a final report worthy of a Pulitzer Prize.

Following is the Final Report more or less as it was presented to the (a) teachers, (b) administrators, (c) superintendent, and (d) school board. A formal presentation was made separately to the first two and last two groups. Overheads of relevant graphics, slides, and a brief "awareness" video about the project were also used. At a year-end "celebration" results were shared with students which stimulated "reflection."

Final Report
Adopt-a-Senior Service-Learning Project
Nurture Primary School, Support County Schools

Executive Summary

An evaluation of an intergenerational service-learning project (Adopt-a-Senior) was conducted in a rural community setting. Participants were 553 prekindergarten through second-grade students and sixty residents of a nursing home. Data were gathered from 313 first- and second-grade students to examine five evaluation questions related to (a) student attitudes toward the elderly, (b) attitudes toward reading, (c) reading achievement, (d) student attitudes toward service-learning, and (e) nursing home residents' evaluation of the intergenerational experience. Major results included:

- statistically significant gains with more positive student attitudes toward the elderly;

- significant gains in student attitudes toward reading. These gains could not, however, be attributed directly to the impact of the program;
- meaningful and statistically significant gains in reading achievement, but not differentially as relative to students who had not participated in the project;
- a moderately positive evaluation by students of the service-learning experience; and
- both positive and negative expression of feelings about the service-learning experience by nursing home residents. Pluses included feelings about having young people look up to them (12 percent) and doing and making things (47 percent). Minuses included fear of not knowing what to expect (15 percent) and difficulty in being able to understand the children (4 percent).

Background/Overview

A year-long project was initiated with $5,500 of state monies (via a federal grant) to establish a service-learning project linking Nurture Primary School and Pine Tree Manor (nursing home). The elderly have a great deal to offer to the youth of our community in terms of experiences and perspective. Our youth also can contribute a great deal to the quality of life of our senior citizens. For the seniors, the project allowed for the sharing of information and wisdom. Student visits provided for a more home-like atmosphere for Pine Tree residents. Student activities were linked to classroom subjects such as writing, reading, mathematics, art, music, and social studies. A formal evaluation of the project was also undertaken.

Project Goals and Evaluation Questions

Three major project goals (PGs) were specified. Associated with these goals were five evaluation questions (EQs) as follows:

PG$_1$: We will facilitate learning between old and young.
  EQ$_1$: Will students engaged in a nursing home service-learning experience change their stereotypical attitudes toward the elderly?

PG$_2$: We will use individual and group talents to help bridge the gap between the generations.
  EQ$_2$: Will students engaged in a nursing home service-learning experience improve their attitudes toward reading?
  EQ$_3$: Will students engaged in a nursing home service-learning experience improve their reading performance?

PG$_3$: We will build character, courtesy, cooperation, and respect among the residents and students.
  EQ$_4$: Will students in a nursing home service-learning experience evaluate their service activity positively?
  EQ$_5$: Will nursing home target participants evaluate their intergenerational experience favorably?

As can be seen, both academic and character education qualities were addressed in the project.

Overview of Treatment

Each month different grade level classes had "responsibilities" for activities and visits to Pine Manor. For example, the second grade had September and February, first grade had October and April, all grades (prekindergarten through second, and continuous progress and special education classes) participated in December activities. Following is a partial list of activities.

- Make fall wreaths
- Put up decorations
- Make decorative flower pots
- Dramatize Johnny Appleseed story

- Make applesauce
- Create turkey centerpiece
- Make placemats
- Make holiday cards
- Make friendship bracelets
- Make picture frames
- Stew crockpot apple treat
- Collect and distribute candy and fruit baskets
- Make photobooks of residents
- Present musical show
- Make windsocks and chimes

All activities had a direct link with the ongoing instructional program.

Description of Targets

A total of 553 students, seventy-five staff members, and thirty classes participated in the school-wide Adopt-a-Senior service-learning project. Students were distributed as follows: PreK = 95; K = 145; 1st = 155; and 2nd = 158. Sixty-three percent of these students qualified for free or reduced breakfast and lunch. There were 149 single-parent homes in the student population.

The sixty residents of Pine Manor nursing home were virtually all female with only nine males present. The average age was seventy-four and there were three Hispanics, twenty-five black, and thirty-two white residents. The average length of residency was slightly over six years.

Instrumentation and Data Collection

The measures associated with each of the evaluation questions and when they were administered is as follows:

Evaluation Question	Instrument	Administration
One: Attitude toward Elderly	Ideas about Young People and Older People	Fall/Spring
Two: Attitude toward Reading	Attitude toward Reading	Fall/Spring
Three: Reading Achievement		Fall/Spring
Four: Attitude toward Service Experience (Students)	Student Service Survey	Spring
Five: Attitude toward Service Experience (Residents)	Survey of Pine Tree Manor residents	Spring

The reader will recall that data collection was limited to first- and second-grade students. The sample sizes for the "target" school were 155 and 158, respectively. Contrast data were available from "comparable" school for seventy-five first and sixty-six second graders. Such contrast data are invaluable and difficult to acquire because the contributing school doesn't gain anything by cooperating as most instruments are treatment-specific.

Limitations

A number of factors could have influenced this project. The direction of those influences is difficult to predict. The school had just implemented a parallel block schedule plan. Just implementing this new way of organizing the instructional program may have adversely affected some of the outcomes. For example, the organization and time devoted to reading activities was modified. Results suggested less than optimal gains in reading performance. Another interfering event was the implementation of an innovation grant aimed at stimulating parents to help children with their schoolwork. An old county school bus (Wheels of Wonder) was refurbished to the tune of $50,000 and equipped with computers, printers, scanners, and all manner and form of educational games and activities. The bus visited six different small cities in the county at convenient locations such as church parking lots and libraries. Parents come onboard to work with a teacher and paraprofessional on instructional activities for their children. How much effect this outreach activity had on Adopt-a-Senior is not known.

Data analyses were limited to first and second graders. This was done for practical reasons. If time and the budget had allowed, interviews with the younger students might have revealed both positive and negative aspects of the program.

Pine Tree Manor Residents may have been overwhelmed by the presence of so many different children, so it may have been difficult to establish a link or bond with the students. Different faces make for different experiences. Different grade levels came at different times, and prekindergartners are quite different from second graders both socially and developmentally. In fact, participation of the prekindergartners was limited. Add to that the fact that kindergartners and prekindergartners are just trying to survive and get ready for the "regular" academic program.

Results

First for consideration is Evaluation Question One, which focused on student attitudes toward the elderly. Scores on the *Ideas about Young People and Older People* attitude scale could range from 18 to 54. Following are the mean and standard deviations for the combined first- and second-grade students in the target and contrast schools from the fall and spring administrations:

	Fall		Spring	
	M	SD	M	SD
Target ($n = 310$)	35.17	5.33	47.51	4.96
Contrast ($n = 137$)	36.30	4.87	38.11	5.28

(See figure 8.1 for a graphic presentation of these data.)

Figure 8.1   Mean Scores on the Ideas about Younger People and Older People Attitude Scale

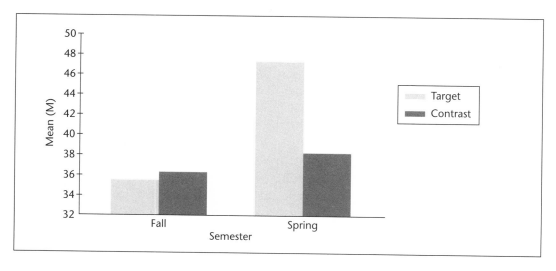

The 12.34 average gain for the target students was statistically significantly different from no gain (p<.01), but the 1.81 average gain for the contrast students was not. The interpretation is that the target students' participation in the service-learning program resulted in a nonchance or nonrandom change in their attitudes about the elderly. Obviously the 12.34 and 1.81 differences were different from each other (p<.01), indicating that the service-learning made the difference. Finally, we can conclude that the effect size (see chapter 7) of 1.78 means that the difference between the target and contrast outcomes was meaningful and practical, and we can have reasonable confidence that engaging in the service-learning program as implemented would again bring about the observed positive changes. No differences between males and females or first and second graders were noted.

Student attitudes toward reading were examined in Evaluation Question Two. Data using the *Attitude toward Reading* (ATR) survey instrument were gathered. The prototype for the ATR in chapter 7 was expanded to fifteen items. Scores on the ATR had a maximum range from 15 to 65. Following are the scores for the target and contrast students for fall and spring. (See figure 8.2 for graphic representation of the results.)

	Fall		Spring	
	M	SD	M	SD
Target	52.36	7.41	60.88	8.37
Contrast	52.64	6.75	59.92	7.58

Although both groups gained in attitude toward reading (8.52 and 7.28 points, respectively), the differences between groups were not meaningful. One reason for this might be that the attitudes were moderately positive to begin with (around 80 percent), so that there was not much "ceiling" on the instrument. Another reason might be that the instrument was not sensitive enough to detect changes. The ATR did have a reliability of .78 (out of a possible 1.00), however, so it was pretty reliable to begin with.

Data collected for the purpose of evaluating student progress in reading (Evaluation Question Three) were derived from the State *Basic Literacy Test*. Since the test was new, existing normative data from the developmental years would not serve as the most relevant benchmark for evaluating results. Cooperation was secured from the contrast school system, and comparison data were obtained. This change from the original evaluation design underscores the "evolutionary" nature of evaluation activities. One must adjust to conditions and make the best of opportunities. Following is a summary of the first- and second-grade results from the 100-point BLT.

Figure 8.2 Mean Scores on the Attitude toward Reading Scale

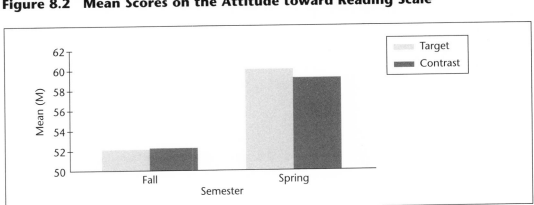

Figure 8.3   Mean Scores on the Georgia State Basic Literacy Test

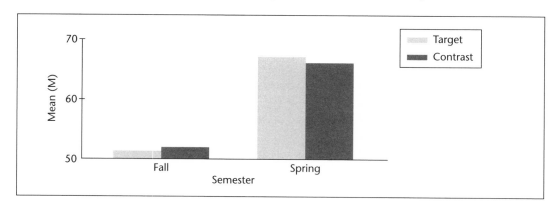

	Fall		Spring	
	M	SD	M	SD
Nurture Elementary				
(*n* = 313)	52.37	8.41	67.53	9.04
Contrast Elementary				
(*n* = 141)	53.48	7.84	66.85	8.11

(See figure 8.3 for a graphic presentation of the data.)

There was significant gain in reading achievement for both groups, but no significant difference between the groups. As noted earlier, reading instruction is heavily emphasized throughout the state, so we're happy for all the children regardless of which group to which they belong.

Evaluation Question Four dealt with student attitudes toward the service experience. The *Student Service Survey* contained fourteen items and used a three-point rating scale. The mean score for spring was 32.46 (standard deviation = 4.23). Given that the maximum possible score was 42, that yields a percent score of 77 percent indicating a moderately high overall positive student evaluation of the experience. The two highest rated items were "Helping others is important" (2.93) and "I think the people at Pine Tree Manor respect me" (2.78). There were no meaningful differences between first and second graders (31.62 vs. 33.30) or between males and females (32.08 vs. 32.84).

The last evaluation question (Five) required information from Pine Tree Manor residents about their experience with the Adopt-a-Senior program. Responses from 32 residents were available from a survey which was administered by the Pine Tree Manor director (see Case Study materials for chapter 6). The four abbreviated survey questions, together with content analyses of the responses, are presented in table 8.2 (percentages of mention).

Having the residents fill out the "Ideas about Young People and Older People" instrument did not prove feasible as the task was too confusing for them: "I keep switching back and forth between them and me."

The old adage about surveying—"If you want to find out what people think, ask them"—is reflected in the residents' responses to the survey. Many excellent suggestions were made for improvement.

Supplementary Findings

Chapter 5 noted that no evaluation question was specifically focused on the development of writing skills. Two sets of relevant information were gathered. The first was the results of administration of the **Do You Like to Write?** instrument to first and second graders. Using the

Table 8.2 Summary of Content Analyses of Pine Tree Manor Survey

Liked Most

Making stuff with them	47%
Being with young people	35%
Doing something different	17%
Having somebody pay attention to me	12%

Liked Least

Not knowing what to expect	15%
So many different kids	10%
Couldn't understand them sometimes	4%
Interfered with my TV programs	2%

What to Change

Have same ones. Always seemed like different kids so couldn't get to know them well.	20%
Have older kids, so can talk with them better	8%
Don't come during mealtimes	5%
Not so many children	

How to Make More Important

Prepare us better	22%

first fourteen items of the Agree-Disagree (Scored Agree = 2, 1 = Disagree) survey, the following data were summarized:

	Nurture Elementary ($n = 310$)		Contrast Elementary ($n = 138$)	
	Fall	Spring	Fall	Spring
Mean	15.38	19.51	13.97	16.11
Standard Deviation	3.41	4.02	4.22	5.14

The gains for Nurture Elementary were statistically significantly greater than for Contrast Elementary. Apparently, at least at the attitude level, there was a meaningful increase in positive feelings about writing. We certainly can't argue cause and effect, but the Contrast Elementary school did not have a systematic service-learning program in place.

The second relevant data set was derived from an analysis of the writing developmental levels derived from the state rubric. Table 8.3 portrays the resulting data (percent in category, September and May).

The data are not dramatic, but there does appear to be a trend toward "improvement" from fall to spring that is somewhat greater for students in Nurture Elementary than in Contrast Elementary. Again, no argument for cause and effect can be made, but the data are perhaps suggestive.

Recommendations

Based on the data available, and after the evaluator's consultations with the project coordinator and the director of the nursing home, the following recommendations were formulated.

- Definitely continue the program next year.
- Limit participants to first and second graders.
- Change the measure of reading achievement.
- Limit visits to mid-morning before lunch.
- Spend an extra week working with residents to prepare them better for the visits.

Table 8.3   Developmental Writing Stage Summary

	Emerg-ing	Develop-ing	Focus-ing	Experi-menting	Engag-ing	Extend-ing
Nurture Elementary						
Fall	44	30	10	14	2	0
Spring	38	22	15	20	4	1
Contrast Elementary						
Fall	51	24	14	10	1	0
Spring	48	31	11	8	2	0

In summary, the service-learning experience had a positive impact on all concerned.

Epilogue: If All Else Fails

If all else fails, use one of the following evaluation models.*

Cosmetic method. You examine the program and if it looks good it is good. Does everybody look busy? The key is attractive and full bulletin boards covered with pictures and pamphlets emanating from the project.

Cardiac method. No matter what the data say, you know in your heart that the program was a success. It is similar to the use of subclinical findings in medical research.

Curricular method. A successful program is one that can be installed with the least disruption of the ongoing school program. Programs that are truly different are to eschewed at all costs.

Computational method. If you have to have data, analyze the hell out of it. No matter the nature of the statistics, use the most sophisticated multivariate regression discontinuity procedures known to humans.

Just kidding!

Appendix A

State Organizations Supporting Service-Learning*

Alabama
Ms. Cyndi Hill Townley
Alabama State Department of Education
50 North Ripley Street, Room 5348
P.O. Box 302101
Montgomery, AL 36104
(334) 353-7001
ctownley@sdenet.alsde.edu

Alaska
Alaska Department of Education
Department of Education and
Early Development
333 W. 4th Avenue, Suite 220
Anchorage, AK 99501
(907) 269-4607

Arizona
Ms. Rogers Jan Brite
Arizona Department of Education
1535 West Jefferson Avenue
Phoenix, AZ 85007
(602) 542-5487
jbrite@maill.ade.state.az.us

California
Mr. Wade S. Brynelson
California Department of Education
721 Capitol Mall
Sacramento, CA 95814
(916) 653-3314
wbrynels@cde.ca.gov

Colorado
Dr. Kate Cumbo
Colorado Department of Education
201 E. Colfax Avenue
Denver, CO 80203
(303) 866-6969
cumbo_k@cde.state.co.us

Connecticut
Ms. Michele Stewart-Copes
Connecticut State Department of Education
165 Capitol Avenue, Room #227
P.O. Box 2219
Hartford, CT 06145
(860) 566-6101
michele.stewart-copes@po.state.ct.us

Delaware
Dr. Margaret S. Dee
Delaware Department of Public Instruction
Delaware Learn and Serve America
P.O. Box 1402
Lockerman Street
Dover, DE 19903-1402
(302) 739-4885
mdee@state.de.us

District of Columbia
Dr. Beverly J. O'Bryant
District of Columbia Public Schools
D. C. Public Schools
825 North Capitol Street, NE, Room 8148
Washington, DC 20002
(202) 442-5155
obryant@k12.dc.us

Florida
Mr. Pete Kreis
Florida Department of Education
325 W. Gaines Street, Suite 126
614 Turlington Boulevard
Tallahassee, FL 32399-0400
(850) 488-1570
alexane2@mail.doe.state.fl.us

*List compiled March 2000.

Georgia
Mr. Richard A. Grover
Georgia Department of Education
1854 Twin Towers East
Atlanta, GA 30334-5040
(404) 657-8335
dgrover@doe.k12.ga.us

Hawaii
Ms. Judy A. McCoy
Hawaii Department of Education
641 18th Avenue, 2nd Floor
Honolulu, HI 96816
(808) 733-9893
judy_mccoy@notes.k12.hi.us

Illinois
Dr. Gary Greene
Illinois State Board of Education
100 W. Randolph Street, Suite 14-300
Chicago, IL 60601
(312) 814-3606
ggreene@smtp.isbe.state.il.us

Indiana
Ms. Evelyn R. Holt Otten
Indiana Department of Education
Office of Program Development
State House 229
Indianapolis, IN 46204-2798
(317) 233-3163
eholt@doe.state.in.us

Iowa
Mr. Joseph P. Herrity
Iowa Department of Education
Grimes State Ofice Building
East 14th and Grand Avenue
Des Moines, IA 50319
(515) 281-3290
joe.herrity@ed.state.ia.us

Kansas
Ms. Rhonda Franke
Kansas Commission on National
and Community Service
120 SE 10th
Topeka, KS 66612
(785) 368-6207
rfranke@ksbe.state.ks.us

Kentucky
Ms. Karen Schmalzbauer
Kentucky Department of Education
1731 Capital Plaza Tower, 500 Mero Street
Frankfort, KY 40601
(502) 564-3678
kschmalz@kde.state.ky.us

Louisiana
Ms. Kay S. Bailey
Louisiana Department of Education
263 Third Street, Suite 610-B
Baton Rouge, LA 70801
(225) 342-3333
kaysbailey@aol.com

Maine
Mr. Edward T. Maroon
Maine Department of Education
23 State House Station
Augusta, ME 04333
(207) 287-5854
ed.maroon@state.me.us

Maryland
Mr. Luke F. Frazier
Maryland State Department of Education
Maryland Student Service Alliance
200 West Baltimore Street
Baltimore, MD 21201
(410) 767-0356
lfrazier@msde.state.md.us

Massachusetts
Ms. Jessica D. Donner
Massachusetts Department of Education
350 Main Street
Malden, MA 02148
(781) 388-3000
jdonner@doe.mass.edu

Michigan
Ms. Barbara R. Knutson
Michigan Department of Education
608 West Allegan
Lansing, MI 48933
(517) 335-0138
knutsonb@state.mi.us

Minnesota
Mr. Carter Hendricks
Minnesota Department of Education
Minnesota Dept. of Children,
Families & Learning
1500 Highway 36 West
Roseville, MN 55113
(651) 582-8307
carter.hendricks@state.mn.us

Mississippi
Ms. Frednia D Perkins
Mississippi Department of Education
P.O. Box 771
500 Greymont Street, Suite H
Jackson, MS 39205-0771
(601) 354-7791
fperkins@mde.k12.ms.us

Missouri
Ms. Karen White
Missouri Department of Elementary
and Secondary Education
P.O. Box 480
205 Jefferson Street
Jefferson City, MO 65109
(573) 526-5395
kwhite3@mail.dese.state.mo.us

Montana
Ms. June Atkins
Montana Department of Education
1300 11th Street
P.O. Box 202501
Helena, MT 59620-2501
(406) 444-3664
jatkins@state.mt.us

Nebraska
Ms. Winona Maxon
Nebraska Department of Education
301 Centennial Mall South, 6th Floor
P.O. Box 94987
Lincoln, NE 68509-4987
(402) 471-4812
wmaxon@edneb.org

Nevada
Ms. Janet Wright
Nevada Department of Education
700 East 5th Street
Carson City, NV 89701-5096
(775) 687-9197
jwright@nsn.k12.nv.us

New Hampshire
Mr. Jayson Seaman
New Hampshire Department of Education
101 Pleasant Street
Concord, NH 03301-3860
(603) 271-3719
jseaman@ed.state.nh.us

New Jersey
Mr. Michael Gowdy
New Jersey Department of Education
100 Riverview Plaza
P.O. Box 500
Trenton, NJ 08625-0500
(609) 777-4612
mgowdy@doe.state.nj.edu

New Mexico
Ms. Carmen E. Endlich
New Mexico Department of Education
300 Don Gaspar
Santa Fe, NM 87501-2786
(505) 476-0195
endlich@sde.state.nm.us

New York
Mr. Stanley S. Hansen, Jr.
New York State Education Department
Bureau of College, School, and
Community Collaboration
Education Building Addition, Room 965
Albany, NY 12234
(518) 486-5202
shansen2@mail.nysed.gov

North Carolina
Dr. Norman C. Camp
North Carolina Department of
Public Instruction
301 North Wilmington Street
Raleigh, NC 27601-2825
(919) 715-1504
ncamp@dpi.state.nc.us

Ohio
Ms. Charlotte Jones-Ward
Ohio Department of Education
65 South Front Street, Room #1009
Columbus, OH 43215-4183
(614) 466-8920
pd_jonesward@ode.ohio.gov

Oklahoma
Mr. Charles Mohr
Oklahoma State Department of Education
2500 North Lincoln Boulevard
Oklahoma, City OK 73105-4599
(405) 521-4795
charles_mohr@mail.sde.state.ok.us

Oregon
Ms. Berverlee Jackson
Oregon Department of Education
Public Service Building
255 Capitol Street, NE
Salem, OR 97310-0203
(503) 378-3584 ext. 369
bev.jackson@state.or.us

Pennsylvania
Ms. Dorothy M. Hershey
Pennsylvania Department of Education
Bureau of Community & Student Services
333 Market Street, 5th Floor
Harrisburg, PA 17126-0333
(717) 783-7089
dhershey@state.pa.us

Rhode Island
Ms. Diana Crowley
Rhode Island Department of Elementary
and Secondary Education
The Shepard Building
255 Westminster Street
Providence, RI 02903
(401) 222 4600 ext. 2167
dcrowley@ride.ri.net

South Carolina
Dr. Kathy Carter
South Carolina Department of Education
1500 Hampton Street, Suite 250B
South Carolina Commission on National
and Community Service, SDE
Columbia, SC 29201
(803) 253-7634
kgibson@sde.state.sc.us

Tennessee
Ms. Jan Bushing
Tennessee Department of Education
Andrew Johnson Tower, 6th Floor
710 James Robertson Parkway
Nashville, TN 37243-0375
(615) 741-0345
jbushing@mail.state.tn.us

Texas
Mr. John Spence
Texas Education Agency
University of Texas at Austin
2613 Speedway, NSAS Annex 1.202
Austin, TX 78712
(512) 232-2291
jspence@mail.utexas.edu

Utah
Mr. Harley E. Paulson
Utah State Office of Education
250 East 500 South
Salt Lake City, UT 84111
(801) 538-7826

Vermont
Mr. Doug Chippetta
Vermont Department of Education
120 State Street
Montpelier, VT 05620-2501
(802) 828-2756
sbailey@doe.state.vt.us

Virginia
Dr. Neils W Brooks
Virginia Office of Volunteerism
P.O.Box 2120
Richmond, VA 23218
(804) 225-3347
nbrooks@pen.k12.va.us

Washington
Gayle Pauley
Washington Department of Education
P.O. Box 47200
Olympia, WA 98504-7200
(360) 853-2858
gpauley@.wednet.edu

West Virginia
Dr. Fred W. Harrington
West Virginia Department of Education
1900 Kanawha Boulevard East
Building 6, Room 230
Charleston, WV 25305-0330
(304) 558-7881
fharring@access.k12.wv.us

Wisconsin
Mr. Jeffery J. Miller
Wisconsin Department of Public Instruction
125 South Webster Street, 5th Floor
P.O. Box 7841
Madison, WI 53707-7841
(608) 261-7494
Jeffery.Miller@dpi.state.wi.us

Wyoming
Kathleen Scheurman
Wyoming Department of Education
Hathaway Building, 2nd Floor
2300 Capitol Avenue
Cheyenne WY 82002-0050
(307) 777-7843
kscheu@educ.state.wy.us

Appendix B

The *Program Evaluation Standards* (1994)

Utility Standards: The utility standards are intended to ensure that an evaluation serves the practical information needs of given audiences. These standards follow.

U1 **Audience Identification.** Audiences involved in or affected by the evaluation should be identified so that their needs can be addressed.

U2 **Evaluator Credibility.** The persons conducting the evaluation should be both trustworthy and competent to perform the evaluation so that their findings achieve maximum credibility and acceptance.

U3 **Information Scope and Selection.** Information collected should be of such scope and selected in such ways as to address pertinent questions about the object of the evaluation and to be responsive to the needs and interests of specified audiences.

U4 **Valuational Interpretation.** The perspectives, procedures, and rationale used to interpret the findings should be carefully described so that the bases for value judgments are clear.

U5 **Report Clarity.** The evaluation report should describe the program being evaluated, including its context, and the purposes, procedures, and findings of the evaluation so that essential information is provided and easily understood.

U6 **Report Timeliness and Dissemination.** Evaluation reports and significant findings should be disseminated to clients and other right-to-know audiences so that they can be used in a timely fashion.

U7 **Evaluation Impact.** Evaluations should be planned, conducted, and reported in ways that encourage follow-through by members of the audiences so that the chances of the evaluation being used are improved.

Feasibility Standards: The feasibility standards are intended to ensure that an evaluation is realistic, prudent, diplomatic, and frugal.

F1 **Practical Procedures.** The evaluation procedures should be practical so that disruption is kept to a minimum and needed information is obtained.

F2 **Political Viability.** The evaluation should be planned and conducted with anticipation of the different positions of various interest groups so that their cooperation may be obtained, and so that possible attempts by any of these groups to curtail evaluation operations or to bias or misapply the results can be averted or counteracted.

F3 **Cost Effectiveness.** The evaluation should produce information of sufficient value so that the expended resources can be justified.

Propriety Standards: The propriety standards are intended to ensure that an evaluation is conducted legally, ethically, and with due regard for the welfare of those involved in the evaluation, as well as those affected by its results.

P1 **Service Orientation.** Evaluations of programs, projects, and materials should be designed to assist organizations to provide services of high quality so that needs of learner development are met.

P2 **Formal Obligations.** Obligations of the formal parties to an evaluation (what is to be done, how, by whom, when) should be agreed to in writing so that these parties are obligated to adhere to all conditions of the agreement or to formally renegotiate it.

P3   **Rights of Human Subjects.** Evaluations should be designed and conducted so that the rights and welfare of the subjects are respected and protected.

P4   **Human Interactions.** Evaluators should respect human dignity and worth in their interactions and with other persons associated with an evaluation so that participants are not harmed or threatened.

P5   **Full and Frank Reporting.** The evaluation should be full and fair in its presentation of strengths and weaknesses of the object being evaluated so that strengths can be built upon and problem areas addressed.

P6   **Disclosure of Findings.** The formal parties to an evaluation should ensure that oral and written evaluation reports are open, correct, and honest in their disclosure of pertinent limitations and findings so that the right to know by persons affected by the evaluation, and any others with express legal rights to see the results, is respected and assured.

P7   **Conflict of Interest.** Conflict of interest, frequently unavoidable, should be dealt with openly and honestly so that it does not compromise evaluation processes and results.

P8   **Fiscal Responsibility.** The evaluator's allocation and expenditure of resources should reflect sound accountability procedures and otherwise be prudent and ethically responsible so that there is no question about how evaluation resources are spent.

Accuracy Standards: The accuracy standards are intended to ensure that an evaluation reveals and conveys technically adequate information about the features that determine worth or merit of the object being evaluated.

A1   **Object Identification.** The object of the evaluation (program, project, material) should be sufficiently examined so that the form(s) of the object being considered in the evaluation can be clearly identified.

A2   **Context Analysis.** The context in which the program, project, or material exists should be examined in enough detail so that its likely influence on the object can be identified.

A3   **Described Purposes and Procedures.** The purposes and procedures of the evaluation should be monitored and described in enough detail so that they can be identified and assessed.

A4   **Defensible Information Sources.** The sources of information should be described in enough detail so that the adequacy of the information can be assessed.

A5   **Valid Measurement.** The data-gathering procedures should be chosen or developed and then implemented in ways that will ensure that the interpretation arrived at is sufficiently reliable for the intended use.

A6   **Reliable Measurement.** The data-gathering procedures should be chosen or developed and then implemented in ways that will ensure that the information obtained is sufficiently reliable for the intended use.

A7   **Systematic Data Control.** The data collected, processed, and reported in an evaluation should be reviewed and corrected so that the results of the evaluation are not flawed.

A8   **Analysis of Quantitative Information.** Quantitative information in an evaluation should be appropriately and systematically analyzed to ensure supportable interpretations.

A9   **Analysis of Qualitative Information.** Qualitative information in an evaluation should be appropriately and systematically analyzed to ensure supportable interpretations.

A10 **Justified Conclusions.** The conclusions reached in an evaluation should be explicitly justified so that the audience can assess them.

A11 **Impartial Reporting.** Reporting procedures should guard against distortion by personal feelings and biases of any party to the evaluation, so that the evaluation reports fairly reflect the evaluation findings.

A12 Meta-evaluation. The evaluation itself should be formatively and summatively evaluated against these and other pertinent standards, so that its conduct is appropriately guided and, on completion, audiences can closely examine its strengths and weaknesses.

Source: The Joint Committee on Standards for Educational Evaluation (1994). *The program evaluation standards* (Second Edition). Thousand Oaks, CA: Sage.

Appendix C

Sample Instrumentation

The following instruments are presented with a strong caveat as they have, in most cases, unknown psychometric support. They are offered to the reader as a starting point for instrument refinement, development, or perhaps to serve as prototypes. Most have been used only two or three times. All may be used and copied without securing permission or making attribution. If, by chance, attributions were overlooked, apologies are hereby made. Copyrighted material has not knowingly been included. The author would like to hear about successes and failures. Virtually all of the instruments are in the affective domain as those seem the hardest to construct.

In addition to the *Mental Measurements Yearbooks* described in chapter 4, the following sources can be very helpful in locating a great variety of psychometric and edumetric measuring instruments.

Chun, K., Cobb, S., & French, Jr., R. P. (1975). *Measures for psychological assessment*. Ann Arbor: Survey Research Center, University of Michigan. (A guide to 3,000 original sources and their applications.)

Directory of selected national testing programs (1987). Phoenix, AZ: Oryx Press.

Educational Testing Service test collection catalogs (1987–200x). Phoenix, AZ: Oryx Press. (Different volumes given over to attitudes, achievement, etc.)

Fabiano, E. (1989). *Index to tests used in educational dissertations*. Phoenix, AZ: Oryx Press.

Goldman, B. A., et al. (1974–1990). *Directory of unpublished experimental measures*. NY: Human Science Press.

Johnson, O. G., & Bommarito, J. W. (1971). *Tests and measurements in child development: A handbook*. San Francisco: Jossey-Bass.

Keyser, D. J., & Sweetland, R. C. (Eds.) (1988). *Test critiques* (Second Edition). Kansas City, MO: Test Corporation of America.

Robinson, J. P., Shaver, P. R., & Wrightsman, L. S. (1991). *Measures of personality and social psychological attitudes*. San Diego: Academic Press.

Shaw, M. E., & Wright, J. M. (1967). *Scales for the measurement of attitudes*. New York: McGraw-Hill.

Walker, D. K. (1973). *Socioemotional measures for preschool and kindergarten children*. San Francisco: Jossey-Bass.

List of Instruments

Attitudes toward School

Please answer each question honestly. Place a check mark ✔ or an X in the space by your choice. Think about each statement before making a choice.

	Yes	Somewhat	No
1. Do you expect school to be an enjoyable place to come for learning?	_____	_____	_____
2. Do you feel that this school is enjoyable?	_____	_____	_____
3. Do you expect to receive good grades in school?	_____	_____	_____
4. Do you receive good grades in school?	_____	_____	_____
5. Do you expect teachers to show you respect and not embarrass you?	_____	_____	_____
6. Do the teachers at this school treat you with respect?	_____	_____	_____
7. Are you involved in a variety of activities at school?	_____	_____	_____
8. Should schools make students feel important?	_____	_____	_____
9. Do you feel like an important member of this school?	_____	_____	_____
10. Should students at a school work to get along well together?	_____	_____	_____
11. Do the students at this school get along well together?	_____	_____	_____
12. Students need to have pride in their school for the school to be a good one.	_____	_____	_____
13. There is a lot of school pride at this school.	_____	_____	_____
14. Teachers should use a variety of activities in class for teaching and keeping students interested.	_____	_____	_____

continued

	Yes	Somewhat	No
15. Teachers at this school use a variety of activities.	___	___	___
16. If I need extra help in class, I should be able to get it.	___	___	___
17. If I am confused in class, I can get help at school.	___	___	___
18. I think my school is attractive and pleasant.	___	___	___
19. This school is a safe place to be.	___	___	___
20. I am happy about coming to school each day.	___	___	___

Student Opinions about School

School _____

Grade   6   7   8
(Circle One)

Dear Student:

Your teachers want to know how you feel about school so they can do a better job. Please tell us how you feel about each of the following statements. *There are no right or wrong answers*, but please tell us how you really feel. Use the following scale

     N = I would *never agree* (or almost never) with this statement.

     S = I would *sometimes agree* with this statement.

     U = I would *usually agree* with this statement.

     A = I would *always agree* (or almost always) with this statement.

Tell us how you really feel.

Thank you

		Never Agree	Sometimes Agree	Usually Agree	Always Agree
1.	Teachers are able to make most subjects interesting.	N	S	U	A
2.	I am good at understanding what the teachers want us to do.	N	S	U	A
3.	I am convinced that school will help me have a better life.	N	S	U	A
4.	If I want to, I can learn most things that are taught in school.	N	S	U	A
5.	I can tell when I am doing well in school.	N	S	U	A
6.	I'm proud of the work I am doing in school.	N	S	U	A
7.	I am enthusiastic about school and look forward to it.	N	S	U	A
8.	I find I have enough time to finish my assigned work in class.	N	S	U	A
9.	I feel satisfied with my grades.	N	S	U	A
10.	I can predict how well I have done on a test before the teacher grades it.	N	S	U	A
11.	I'm not at all sure how to please my teachers.	N	S	U	A

continued

		Never Agree	Sometimes Agree	Usually Agree	Always Agree
12.	Most of the things we do in school are easy for me.	N	S	U	A
13.	Homework is really important, so I make sure that I get all of it done.	N	S	U	A
14.	My schoolwork and special projects are put on display for others to see.	N	S	U	A
15.	The harder the schoolwork, the more interesting it is for me.	N	S	U	A
16.	When a teacher is absent, I don't bother to do any work.	N	S	U	A
17.	I notice that when my friends don't come to school, I don't want to come either.	N	S	U	A
18.	My life at school is completely out of my control.	N	S	U	A
19.	The good teachers are the ones who expect the highest-quality work.	N	S	U	A
20.	I am skillful at learning new, different subjects.	N	S	U	A
21.	I try to get really involved in all of my subjects.	N	S	U	A
22.	School is where I became aware of my abilities.	N	S	U	A
23.	I feel comfortable using computers in class.	N	S	U	A
24.	My teachers are always trying out new ways to teach things.	N	S	U	A
25.	In each class I use information from other classes.	N	S	U	A
26.	It takes effort to learn with computers.	N	S	U	A
27.	Computers help me better understand my schoolwork.	N	S	U	A
28.	If I learn with computers, it helps me remember more information.	N	S	U	A
29.	Computers help me solve problems.	N	S	U	A
30.	Computers make learning more life-like.	N	S	U	A

Environmental Attitudes*

Teacher _____   Name _____

Date _____

Grade _____

Male   Female

(Circle one)

Please read each statement and decide if you agree or disagree with it. Simply indicate how you really feel by circling an "A" or "D." There are no right or wrong answers.

1.	I would be willing to stop buying some products to save animals' lives.	A	D
2.	I would *not* be willing to save energy by using less air conditioning.	A	D
3.	To save water, I would be willing to use less water when I bathe.	A	D
4.	I would *not* give my own money to help the environment.	A	D
5.	I would be willing to ride the bus to more places to help reduce air pollution.	A	D
6.	I would *not* be willing to separate my family's trash for recycling.	A	D
7.	I would give my own money to help protect wild animals.	A	D
8.	To save energy, I would be willing to use dimmer light bulbs.	A	D
9.	To save water, I would be willing to turn off the water while I wash my hands.	A	D
10.	I would go from house to house to pass out environmental information.	A	D
11.	I would be willing to write letters asking people to help reduce pollution.	A	D
12.	I would be willing to go from house to house asking people to recycle.	A	D
13.	I have *not* written someone about a pollution problem.	A	D

continued

*Based on ideas in Maloney, M. P., Ward, M. P., & Broucht, G. N. (1975). A revised scale for the measurement of ecological attitudes and knowledge. *American Psychologist*, 30, 787–790; and Leeming, F. C., Dwyer, W. O., & Bracken, B. A. (1995). Children's environmental attitude and knowledge scale: Construction and validation. *Journal of Environmental Education*, 26(3), 22–31.

14. I have talked with my parents about how to help with environmental problems.   A   D

15. I turn off the water in the sink while I brush my teeth to conserve water.   A   D

16. To save energy, I turn off lights at home when they are not in use.   A   D

17. I have asked my parents not to buy products made from animal fur.   A   D

18. I have asked my family to recycle some of the things we use.   A   D

19. I have asked others what I can do to help reduce pollution.   A   D

20. I often read stories that are mostly about the environment.   A   D

21. I do *not* let a water faucet run when it is not necessary.   A   D

22. I leave the refrigerator door open while I decide what to get out.   A   D

23. I have put up a birdhouse near my home.   A   D

24. I do *not* separate things at home for recycling.   A   D

25. I am frightened to think that people don't care about the environment.   A   D

26. I get angry about the damage pollution does to the environment.   A   D

27. It makes me happy when people recycle used bottles, cans, and paper.   A   D

28. I get angry when I think about companies testing products on animals.   A   D

29. It makes me happy to see people trying to save energy.   A   D

30. I am *not* worried about running out of water.   A   D

31. I do *not* worry about environmental problems.   A   D

32. I am *not* frightened about the effects of pollution on my family.   A   D

33. I get upset when I think of the things people throw away that could be recycled.   A   D

34. It makes me sad to see houses being built where animals used to live.   A   D

35. It frightens me to think how much energy is wasted.   A   D

36. It upsets me when I see people use too much water.   A   D

_____
(Grade)

_____
(School)

_____
(Date)

Student Attitudes about the Study of Geography

Directions: Please read each statement and decide if you feel *Very Positive, Positive, Negative,* or *Quite Negative* about it, or *Can't Decide. Please* take this task seriously as only then can the results be meaningful.

	My Feelings about this Statement				
	Very Positive	Positive	Can't Decide (Circle One)	Negative	Quite Negative
1. I feel good about my knowledge about geography.	VP	P	CD	N	QN
2. We should learn more about geography.	VP	P	CD	N	QN
3. Knowing about other lands and places doesn't help us at home.	VP	P	CD	N	QN
4. Geography should be taught as a separate subject.	VP	P	CD	N	QN
5. I know more about foreign lands and people than my fellow students do.	VP	P	CD	N	QN
6. It is important for students to understand the concepts of geography.	VP	P	CD	N	QN
7. Maps help us learn about many different things.	VP	P	CD	N	QN
8. A strong relationship exists between geography and other subject areas.	VP	P	CD	N	QN
9. It is important for students to recognize the role of geography in current events.	VP	P	CD	N	QN
10. Too much school time is spent on geography.	VP	P	CD	N	QN
11. Geography is as important as any school subject.	VP	P	CD	N	QN
12. Computers are a great help in studying geography.	VP	P	CD	N	QN

_____
(Grade)

_____
(School)

Feelings about My School

This is not a test. Your teacher will read some statements about how you feel things went in school this year. After you hear each statement decide if it was true for you *most of the time, some of the time,* or *almost never.* Circle your choice for each statement and tell us how you really feel.

Draw a Circle around your answer.

For Example:
    Students like to draw.   (Most of the Time)   Some of the Time   Almost Never

This student thought that students like to draw MOST OF THE TIME.

	Most of the Time	Some of the Time	Almost Never
1. Students like coming to school.	Most of the Time	Some of the Time	Almost Never
2. Students get into trouble in the hallways.	Most of the Time	Some of the Time	Almost Never
3. Our teachers help with schoolwork.	Most of the Time	Some of the Time	Almost Never
4. Parents help with homework.	Most of the Time	Some of the Time	Almost Never
5. Students like to learn how to write.	Most of the Time	Some of the Time	Almost Never
6. Students get into trouble in the school yard.	Most of the Time	Some of the Time	Almost Never
7. Our teachers like coming to school.	Most of the Time	Some of the Time	Almost Never
8. Students like to solve problems.	Most of the Time	Some of the Time	Almost Never
9. Students like to work with other students on projects.	Most of the Time	Some of the Time	Almost Never
10. Students like to learn how to read.	Most of the Time	Some of the Time	Almost Never

11. Each student wants to do better than all the other students.	Most of the Time	Some of the Time	Almost Never
12. Parents know how their children are doing in school.	Most of the Time	Some of the Time	Almost Never
13. Students like to help other students.	Most of the Time	Some of the Time	Almost Never
14. Students in my school get into trouble in the lunchroom.	Most of the Time	Some of the Time	Almost Never
15. Students like to learn how to work with numbers.	Most of the Time	Some of the Time	Almost Never

_____
(Grade)

_____
(School)

Feelings about My School
(Retrospective Survey)

This is not a test. Your teacher will read questions to you to find out how you think school went this year compared with last year. If there is no difference between this year and last year, it was about the *same*. Think before you answer and tell us how you really feel.

Draw a Circle around your answer.

For Example:
   Students like to draw.   (More THIS year)   More LAST year   SAME

This student thought that students like to draw more *this* year than *last* year.

1. Students like coming to school.	More THIS year	More LAST year	SAME
2. Students get into trouble in the hallways.	More THIS year	More LAST year	SAME
3. Our teachers help with schoolwork.	More THIS year	More LAST year	SAME
4. Parents help with homework.	More THIS year	More LAST year	SAME
5. Students like to learn how to write.	More THIS year	More LAST year	SAME
6. Students get into trouble in the school yard.	More THIS year	More LAST year	SAME
7. Our teachers like coming to school.	More THIS year	More LAST year	SAME
8. Students like to solve problems.	More THIS year	More LAST year	SAME
9. Students like to work with other students on projects.	More THIS year	More LAST year	SAME
10. Students like to learn how to read.	More THIS year	More LAST year	SAME

11.	Each student wants to do better than all the other students.	More THIS year	More LAST year	SAME
12.	Parents know how their children are doing in school.	More THIS year	More LAST year	SAME
13.	Students in my school like to help other students.	More THIS year	More LAST year	SAME
14.	Students are sent to the principal's office.	More THIS year	More LAST year	SAME
15.	Students in my school get into trouble in the lunchroom.	More THIS year	More LAST year	SAME
16.	Students like to learn how to work with numbers.	More THIS year	More LAST year	SAME

The "Helping Others" Survey

Following are some statements about how people feel about other people. Please read each statement and decide how much you agree or disagree with it, then circle your choice next to the statement.

If you can't decide, circle the question mark (?).

Obviously there are no right or wrong answers, so please express how you really feel.

		Disagree		**?**	**Agree**	
1.	It is important to give to charity.	a Lot	a Little	?	a Lot	a Little
2.	People should be accepting of other people.	a Lot	a Little	?	a Lot	a Little
3.	Being interested in people feels good.	a Lot	a Little	?	a Lot	a Little
4.	The "Golden Rule" really doesn't work.	a Lot	a Little	?	a Lot	a Little
5.	We should visit sick people.	a Lot	a Little	?	a Lot	a Little
6.	Turning the other cheek is silly.	a Lot	a Little	?	a Lot	a Little
7.	It is more blessed to give than to receive.	a Lot	a Little	?	a Lot	a Little
8.	Everyone should help those who are worse off than they are.	a Lot	a Little	?	a Lot	a Little
9.	You don't always have to be generous.	a Lot	a Little	?	a Lot	a Little
10.	Children should run errands for older people.	a Lot	a Little	?	a Lot	a Little
11.	Hospitality is a way of life in our home.	a Lot	a Little	?	a Lot	a Little
12.	Students should be willing to share their lunch with a friend.	a Lot	a Little	?	a Lot	a Little
13.	Helping a friend with homework is OK.	a Lot	a Little	?	a Lot	a Little
14.	Listening to someone else's troubles is part of being a good friend.	a Lot	a Little	?	a Lot	a Little

I am in the _____ grade.

I am a _____ male _____ female.

Ways of Behaving Survey

In the following questionnaire you are presented with more or less familiar situations and are asked to rank three ways of behaving.

Rank each of the behaviors as follows:

Rank 1 = Something I would most likely do

Rank 2 = Something I might do

Rank 3 = Something I would *not* likely do

So far as possible, base your answer on what you actually would do in these situations. Remember! This information will remain confidential!

Example: As you start to cross the street a car stops directly in front of you. As you walk around the car, you would:
a) shout at the driver.   3
b) give him a dirty look.   2
c) do nothing.   1

If you answer as shown above, then you would most likely do nothing, and most probably would not shout at the driver.

Rank 1 = Something I would most likely do

Rank 2 = Something I might do

Rank 3 = Something I would *not* likely do

Situations

1. If you were asked to contribute to a charity with which you are only vaguely familiar, you would:
   a) not contribute.   _____
   b) probably give something.   _____
   c) contribute as much as you can.   _____

2. If you were sitting in the bus and another passenger discovers that he has no money for the fare, you would:
   a) pay his fare for him.   _____
   b) lend him a couple of dollars to make sure he had some money in his pocket.   _____
   c) not worry about it since the conductor will probably let him go by.   _____

3. If one of your friends were sick for a period of time you would:
   a) just send him a card.   _____
   b) try to find out how he is doing every once in a while.   _____
   c) go over to his house daily and help him catch up with school.   _____

continued

4. If an acquaintance who was looking for a job came to you for
   help, you would:
   a) refer him to some agency. _____
   b) help him search the newspaper. _____
   c) try all possible connections and not give up until you've
      found him a job. _____

5. If you had lent somebody money who promised to give it
   back but who still needs it, but you need it also, you would:
   a) demand it back immediately. _____
   b) make some remark to the effect that you need the money. _____
   c) try to get money somewhere else. _____

6. If a student borrowed something of yours (like a book) without
   asking because he needed it for a term paper, you would:
   a) tell him he could have it any time it was not being used. _____
   b) make him return it because he took it without asking. _____
   c) let him have it if you did not need it, but tell him to ask
      you the next time. _____

7. If one of your classmates were in danger of failing a course
   and he asked you to help him out a little during an examination, you would:
   a) tell him that you are sorry but you don't cheat. _____
   b) not help him cheat but give him a good pep talk to raise
      his confidence. _____
   c) tell him that he should be ashamed of himself for trying
      to cheat. _____

8. If you were studying for an examination for the next day, and
   an acquaintance of yours drops by to discuss a personal problem
   with you, you would:
   a) explain to him that you have to study for an exam, but that
      you would see him after the exam. _____
   b) try to help him with his problems. _____
   c) tell him to leave you alone. _____

9. If you were given one wish that would come true, you would
   wish for:
   a) a lot of money. _____
   b) brotherhood of all nations. _____
   c) health and happiness for you and your family. _____

10. If you owned a car and you knew that an acquaintance of yours,
    who does not own a car, had to move, you would:
    a) offer to help him move with your car. _____
    b) help him move if he asked you to. _____
    c) try to avoid using your car for moving Purposes. _____

I am in the _____ grade.
I am a _____ male _____ female.

Ways of Behaving (Key)

1. a) 3
    b) 2
    c) 1

2. a) 2
    b) 1
    c) 3

3. a) 3
    b) 2
    c) 1

4. a) 3
    b) 2
    c) 1

5. a) 3
    b) 2
    c) 1

6. a) 1
    b) 3
    c) 2

7. a) 2
    b) 1
    c) 3

8. a) 2
    b) 1
    c) 3

9. a) 3
    b) 1
    c) 2

10. a) 1
    b) 2
    c) 3

Scoring (High Score = More altruistic)

Match of First choice	=	3
Match of Second choice	=	2
Match of Third choice	=	1
Max. score on any item	=	6
Min. score on any item	=	0
Max. total score	=	60
Min. total score	=	0

Thoughts about Responsibility Survey*

We are interested in finding out about how students feel about how people get along with each other. Read each statement carefully and then circle the phrase that expresses the degree to which you agree or disagree with it.

Please Express How You Really Feel

1. It is no use worrying about current events or public affairs; I can't do anything about them anyway.

    Strongly Agree   Agree   Undecided   Disagree   Strongly   Disagree

2. Everyone should give some of their time for the good of their town or country.

    Strongly Agree   Agree   Undecided   Disagree   Strongly   Disagree

3. Our country would be a lot better off if we didn't have so many elections and people didn't have to vote so often.

    Strongly Agree   Agree   Undecided   Disagree   Strongly   Disagree

4. Letting your friends down is not so bad because you can't do good for everybody all the time.

    Strongly Agree   Agree   Undecided   Disagree   Strongly   Disagree

5. It is the duty of each person to do his job the very best he can.

    Strongly Agree   Agree   Undecided   Disagree   Strongly   Disagree

6. People would be a lot better off if they could live far away from other people and never have to do anything for them.

    Strongly Agree   Agree   Undecided   Disagree   Strongly   Disagree

7. At school I usually volunteer for special projects.

    Strongly Agree   Agree   Undecided   Disagree   Strongly   Disagree

8. I feel very bad when I have failed to finish a job I promised I would do.

    Strongly Agree   Agree   Undecided   Disagree   Strongly   Disagree

I am in the _____ grade.
I am a _____ male _____ female.

*Based on ideas contained in Berkowitz, L., & Lutterman, K. (1968). The traditionally socially responsible personality. *Public Opinion Quarterly, 32,* 169–185.

SOUTH CAROLINA LEARN AND SERVE*
Local School-Based Programs
High School & Junior High/Middle School
School Student Survey

This survey will be kept confidential. Please do not sign your name or make a direct reference to any individual.

Sex: _____ Race (optional): _____ Age: _____ Grade: _____

School you attend: _____

Classes in which you participate in Service-Learning Activities: _____

_____

Please write a brief definition of Service-Learning as you understand it: _____

_____

Please circle the number that best describes your thoughts about each statement.
6 = Strongly Agree; 5 = Somewhat Agree; 4 = Agree; 3 = Neutral; 2 = Somewhat Disagree; 1 = Strongly Disagree; Blank = Cannot Rate

Service-Learning Activities:

1.	Acquaint me with career possibilities.	1	2	3	4	5	6
2.	Broaden my understanding of places and people.	1	2	3	4	5	6
3.	Develop personal qualities in me such as confidence and self-reliance.	1	2	3	4	5	6
4.	Help me acquire new skills, interests, and knowledge.	1	2	3	4	5	6
5.	Help me to form habits of community service and volunteerism.	1	2	3	4	5	6
6.	Help me understand better what I study in class.	1	2	3	4	5	6
7.	Give me an opportunity to be creative and see my ideas put to work.	1	2	3	4	5	6
8.	Help me to better understand my community and how it works.	1	2	3	4	5	6
9.	Teach me how to work better on a team.	1	2	3	4	5	6
10.	Build school spirit.	1	2	3	4	5	6
11.	Should be worked into all of my classes.	1	2	3	4	5	6
12.	Make learning more interesting.	1	2	3	4	5	6
13.	Help me to see how what I study is connected to my life outside of school.	1	2	3	4	5	6

*Reproduced by permission of Dr. Kathy Carter, Service-Learning Coordinator, South Carolina Department of Education.

SOUTH CAROLINA LEARN AND SERVE*
Local School-Based Programs
Elementary School Student Survey

This survey will be kept confidential. Please do not sign your name or make a direct reference to any individual.

Sex: _____   Race (optional): _____   Age: _____   Grade: _____

School you attend: _____

Classes in which you participate in Service-Learning Activities: _____

_____

What does Service-Learning mean to you?: _____

_____

Please circle the number that best describes your thoughts about each statement.
6 = Strongly Agree; 5 = Somewhat Agree; 4 = Agree; 3 = Neutral; 2 = Somewhat Disagree; 1 = Strongly Disagree; Blank = Cannot Rate

Service-Learning Activities:

1.	Teach me about interesting jobs.	1	2	3	4	5	6
2.	Introduce me to new people and places.	1	2	3	4	5	6
3.	Make me feel good about myself and believe in myself.	1	2	3	4	5	6
4.	Teach me new things.	1	2	3	4	5	6
5.	Make me want to volunteer more.	1	2	3	4	5	6
6.	Help me understand what I study in class better.	1	2	3	4	5	6
7.	Let me be creative and use my own ideas.	1	2	3	4	5	6
8.	Help me to better understand my community and how it works.	1	2	3	4	5	6
9.	Teach me how to work better with my classmates.	1	2	3	4	5	6
10.	Build school spirit.	1	2	3	4	5	6
11.	Should be part of all of my classes.	1	2	3	4	5	6
12.	Make learning more interesting.	1	2	3	4	5	6
13.	Help me see how what I study is connected to my life outside of school.	1	2	3	4	5	6

*Reproduced by permission of Dr. Kathy Carter, Service-Learning Coordinator, South Carolina Department of Education.

The Volunteer Survey

Name of Site _____ Date _____

Name of Student Evaluator _____ Grade _____

Supervisor's Name _____

Number of Weeks at Site _____ Number of Hours Per Week at Site _____

Please rate the following categories about your volunteer site on a scale from a very sad to very happy face.

1. I enjoy volunteer work?

2. I would tell others to volunteer?

3. My volunteer work is fun?

4. I get along well with my supervisor?

5. I think adults respect me?

6. The volunteer work I do is important?

7. I am learning new skills?

8. I am learning things that could help me in the future?

9. I have a lot of responsibility at my volunteer job?

10. My work is appreciated?

11. I want to do a good job at my volunteer site?

12. I am helping to improve my community?

Georgia Survey of Attitude toward Service*

Name _____ Grade _____ School _____

Directions: Put a check ✔ in the box that is closest to how *you* feel.	Strongly Agree	Agree	In Between	Disagree	Strongly Disagree
1. Everyone should give some of his or her time for the good of their town.					
2. Kids should never help out for free if there are grown-ups who are paid to do the same job.					
3. It is better for prisoners to pick up trash along the highway than for students to do it.					
4. I feel bad when I don't finish a job I promised I would do.					
5. Helping younger students with their schoolwork would be a waste of my time.					
6. It might be fun to work as a volunteer for awhile in another country.					
7. It would be embarrassing to ask strangers to give money to charity.					
8. I would like to spend one Saturday a month collecting food for homeless people.					

*Developed by Dr. Michael McKenna, Georgia Southern University.

	Strongly Agree	Agree	In Between	Disagree	Strongly Disagree
9. I would feel good about doing a chore for an elderly person.					
10. It is my duty to help recycle paper and cans.					
11. People who volunteer are usually trying to impress somebody.					
12. If you do a good job helping others, you should be paid.					
13. I would enjoy planting flowers or trees to make my school more beautiful.					
14. It would make me feel good to give my old clothes to poor children.					
15. I would enjoy listening to a younger student read.					
16. I would like to deliver food baskets to poor families at Thanksgiving.					
17. Needy people have no one but themselves to blame for their troubles.					
18. Kids who do chores at home should be paid.					

Reflections on Service-Learning Activity*

What insights did I gain from this experience?

How well did I perform my task?

How well did I cooperate with others?

What did I learn from this experience?

What problem(s) did I encounter that I overcame?

How could I have improved this experience?

What were the good qualities of this experience?

What were the qualities that could be changed to make this a better experience?

*Davis, K. M., Miller, M. D., & Corbett, W. (1997). *Methods of evaluating student performance through service-learning*. Gainesville, FL: P. K. Yonge Developmental Research School, College of Education, University of Florida.

Service-Learning Performance Checklist*

Supervisor's Name: _____

Placement: _____

Student's Name: _____

Advisor: _____

Please list the specific activities in which the student has been involved and the skills that were practiced/learned:

Please update the student's performance below using the following letter codes

E = Excellent   VG = Very Good   S = Satisfactory   LS = Less than Satisfactory

	Supervisor or Advisor	Student
Attendance/Punctuality:		
Is consistent in attendance	_____	_____
Reports to community site on time	_____	_____
Attitude:		
Accepts responsibility	_____	_____
Is enthusiastic and interested	_____	_____
Displays appropriate appearance and dress	_____	_____
Is courteous and cooperative	_____	_____
Displays emotional maturity	_____	_____
Exercises good judgment	_____	_____
Is sincere	_____	_____
Relates well to a variety of people	_____	_____
Learning Process:		
Shows initiative	_____	_____
Assumes responsibility for own learning	_____	_____
Asks appropriate questions	_____	_____
Performances:		
Begins work promptly	_____	_____
Appreciates suggestions	_____	_____
Completes assigned tasks	_____	_____
Exhibits competence	_____	_____
Progressively requires less supervision	_____	_____
Is a dependable worker	_____	_____
Follows directions carefully	_____	_____

*Adapted from Central Park East Secondary School's Community Service-Learning Program.

Student Perceptions of Service-Learning Activities*

Dear Student: For each sentence below, please indicate by circling whether you *Strongly Agree* (SA), *Agree* (A), *Disagree* (D), *Strongly Disagree* (SD), or *Don't Know* (DK) that it is true about you.

Because of my involvement with service-learning projects at school this year I . . .

1.	have improved my behavior at school.	DK	SD	D	A	SA
2.	have improved my behavior at home.	DK	SD	D	A	SA
3.	accept more responsibility at school.	DK	SD	D	A	SA
4.	accept more responsibility at home.	DK	SD	D	A	SA
5.	accept more responsibility in my community.	DK	SD	D	A	SA
6.	feel better about myself.	DK	SD	D	A	SA
7.	have developed new skills that I use at school.	DK	SD	D	A	SA
8.	have developed new skills that I use at home.	DK	SD	D	A	SA
9.	have developed new skills that I use in my community.	DK	SD	D	A	SA
10.	am more able to apply academic skills to real-world situations at school.	DK	SD	D	A	SA
11.	am more able to apply academic skills to real-world situations at home.	DK	SD	D	A	SA
12.	am more motivated to attend school.	DK	SD	D	A	SA
13.	am more motivated at home.	DK	SD	D	A	SA
14.	have used information learned in service-learning to plan educational goals.	DK	SD	D	A	SA
15.	have used information learned in service-learning to plan career goals.	DK	SD	D	A	SA
16.	have developed more concern for people, the community, or the environment.	DK	SD	D	A	SA
17.	have discovered or developed leadership skills.	DK	SD	D	A	SA
18.	am more able to work in a cooperative group.	DK	SD	D	A	SA
19.	have become more involved in extracurricular activities.	DK	SD	D	A	SA
20.	have a better understanding of how school learning relates to future work and lifestyles.	DK	SD	D	A	SA

*Adapted by Dr. Steve Cramer, University of Georgia, from materials originated by the Florida Department of Education.

On the lines below, please list up to three Service-Learning projects that you participated in. To the **left** of your list, please rate the project in terms of how **meaningful they were to you**, where 5 means *Very Meaningful* and 1 means *Couldn't Care Less*. To the **right** of your list, please rate the project in terms of how much **impact you had on the service recipient**, where 5 means *Great Impact* and 1 means *No Impact*.

Meaningful		**Impact**
1 2 3 4 5	(1) _____	1 2 3 4 5
1 2 3 4 5	(2) _____	1 2 3 4 5
1 2 3 4 5	(3) _____	1 2 3 4 5

Did the project(s) help you apply something you had learned in an academic subject? (Please circle)

Yes   No

Were any of the project(s) used as a club activity? (Please circle)

Yes   No

Which one(s) _____

What part of the Service-Learning experience meant the most to you? (Check all that apply.)

_____ Learning about the project
_____ Planning the project
_____ Participating in the service
_____ Reflecting on the service and learning
_____ Celebrating
_____ Moving on to the next step
_____ Other _____

What Service-Learning activities did you like the least?

Do you have suggestions for improving the Service-Learning program? If so, write them here.

Thank you for your feedback.

Grade of my child _____

School _____

School Survey

Dear Parent/Guardian:

As the school year begins to come to a close, the teachers and administration of your child's school are interested in finding out how good a job you think we have done this year. The information will help us do an even better job next year.

Please take a few minutes and enter a check mark for each judgment about your satisfaction about each statement. The results will be summarized and a report shared at a later date.

Thank you for sharing your opinions!

	My Satisfaction Is		
	High	**Moderate**	**Low**
1. My child's overall progress in school	_____	_____	_____
2. The climate for learning in my child's school	_____	_____	_____
3. The educational standards of my child's school	_____	_____	_____
4. The way students are assigned to classrooms	_____	_____	_____
5. How well the school motivates my child to do well	_____	_____	_____
6. How well my child gets along with other children	_____	_____	_____
7. How well the school staff treats my child	_____	_____	_____
8. How well the teachers maintain discipline in the classroom	_____	_____	_____
9. The quality of teaching in our school	_____	_____	_____
10. How well my child likes his or her teachers	_____	_____	_____
11. The amount of information I receive about school activities	_____	_____	_____
12. The reports I get about my child's progress in school	_____	_____	_____
13. Relations between parents and the staff in my child's school	_____	_____	_____
14. The way in which the school deals with my child's strengths and weaknesses	_____	_____	_____
15. How well the school helps my child learn to get along with others	_____	_____	_____

Grade of my child _____

School _____

Elementary School Survey
(Retrospective Version)

Dear Parent/Guardian:

As the school year begins to come to a close, the teachers and administration of the school would like your opinion of how well we performed in working with your child this year. The information will help us do an even better job next year.

Please take a few minutes to make a judgment about each statement and return this form to the school. The results will be summarized and a report shared at a later date.

Important: Only parents/guardians with children in grade(s) one, two, or three should respond to this survey.

Thank you for sharing your opinions!

	Better This Year	**Better Last Year**	**No Difference**
1. My child's overall progress in school	_____	_____	_____
2. The climate for learning in my child's school	_____	_____	_____
3. The educational standards of my child's school	_____	_____	_____
4. The way students are assigned to classrooms	_____	_____	_____
5. How well the school motivates my child to do well	_____	_____	_____
6. How well my child gets along with other children	_____	_____	_____
7. How well the school staff treats my child	_____	_____	_____
8. How well the teachers maintain discipline in the classroom	_____	_____	_____
9. The quality of teaching in our school	_____	_____	_____
10. How well my child likes his or her teachers	_____	_____	_____

Service-Learning Teacher Survey

As you know, we have had a grant from the State Department of Education to implement some service-learning projects in our school this year. Please take a couple of minutes to share some of your thoughts about that experience. Please return anonymously to the principal. Many thanks!

1. What do you think were the major benefits to the students resulting from their service-learning experience?

2. What benefits did you derive from the service-learning experience?

3. Should service-learning activities be continued in our school? Why or why not?

4. If these activities are continued, what should we do differently?

5. Have you changed your teaching methods as a result of your service-learning experience? If yes, in what way?

6. What were the negatives, if any, of your service-learning experience?

Survey of School Staff Opinions

Dear Colleague:

I'm sure you will agree that lots of things have happened both in and out of the classroom that have influenced our school this year. The school year is drawing to a close. We very much need your cooperation so that we may fulfill our obligation to the State Department of Education from which we received our funding. Circle your choice for each statement; please respond to each item. *No names please.* A summary will be made available as soon as possible.

Many, many thanks!

	Better This Year	Better Last Year	No Difference
1. The extent to which school policy is communicated to staff	BTY	BLY	ND
2. The extent to which school goals are communicated to parents	BTY	BLY	ND
3. Staff feelings about or ownership of school mission and goals	BTY	BLY	ND
4 Extent of staff input in determining school mission and goals	BTY	BLY	ND
5. Extent to which parents are committed to attainment of school goals	BTY	BLY	ND
6. Extent to which school discipline policies and procedures are clearly stated	BTY	BLY	ND
7. Security and comfort of the school building	BTY	BLY	ND
8. Maintenance of school buildings and grounds	BTY	BLY	ND
9. Classroom management and discipline	BTY	BLY	ND
10. Administration of discipline policies and procedures	BTY	BLY	ND
11. School staff expectation that students can master basic skills	BTY	BLY	ND
12. Extent to which staff members are encouraged to improve themselves professionally	BTY	BLY	ND
13. Teacher feelings of accountability			
14. Extent to which high expectations for students are communicated to them	BTY	BLY	ND
15. Extent to which high expectations for students are communicated to parents	BTY	BLY	ND
16. Extent to which I look forward to coming to work	BTY	BLY	ND
17. Extent to which school personnel are involved in decision making	BTY	BLY	ND
18. Degree of mutual respect among students, teachers, and administrators	BTY	BLY	ND
19. Staff accomplishments formally and informally recognized	BTY	BLY	ND

Parent Perceptions of Students Involved in Service-Learning Activities*

Your student has participated in the Service-Learning Program at school. We are trying to find out how participating in Service-Learning helps students. You can help us by answering the questions below. You do not need to sign this survey.

For each sentence below, please indicate by circling whether you *Strongly Agree* (SA), *Agree* (A), *Disagree* (D), *Strongly Disagree* (SD), or *Don't Know* (DK) that it is true for your student.

Because of his or her involvement with Service-Learning projects at school this year, my student . . .

1.	Accepts more responsibility at home	SA	A	D	SD	DK
2.	Talks with me about his/her Service-Learning activities	SA	A	D	SD	DK
3.	Demonstrates more positive self-esteem at home	SA	A	D	SD	DK
4.	Is more able to apply academic skills to real-world situations at home	SA	A	D	SD	DK
5.	Is more motivated at home	SA	A	D	SD	DK
6.	Is more motivated within the community	SA	A	D	SD	DK
7.	Is more motivated to attend school	SA	A	D	SD	DK
8.	Has used information learned in Service-Learning to plan educational goals	SA	A	D	SD	DK
9.	Has used information learned in Service-Learning to plan career goals	SA	A	D	SD	DK
10.	Has shown increased concern for people, the community, or the environment	SA	A	D	SD	DK
11.	Is more interested in volunteer activities	SA	A	D	SD	DK
12.	Did your student's Service-Learning experience help his/her academic achievement?	SA	A	D	SD	DK

Yes   No

Why or why not?

13. Would you be interested in participating in a Service-Learning project with the school? If so, please write your name and phone number below.

Name _____ Phone _____

Thank you for your feedback

*Adapted by Dr. Steve Cramer, University of Georgia, from material originated by the Florida State Department of Education.

Teacher Perceptions of Students Involved in Service-Learning Activities*

For each sentence below, please indicate by circling whether you *Strongly Agree* (SA), *Agree* (A), *Disagree* (D), *Strongly Disagree* (SD), or *Don't Know* (DK) that it is true for your students who have been involved in Service-Learning projects.

Because of their involvement with service-learning projects at school, my students . . .

1.	Have demonstrated more acceptable classroom behavior	SA	A	D	SD	DK
2.	Are more motivated at school	SA	A	D	SD	DK
3.	Accept more responsibility at school	SA	A	D	SD	DK
4.	Demonstrate a more positive self-image at school	SA	A	D	SD	DK
5.	Have developed new academic skills	SA	A	D	SD	DK
6.	Have developed new interpersonal skills	SA	A	D	SD	DK
7.	Have raised classroom grades	SA	A	D	SD	DK
8.	Have reduced absences and tardies	SA	A	D	SD	DK
9.	Have reduced discipline referrals	SA	A	D	SD	DK
10.	Are more able to apply academic skills to real-world situations	SA	A	D	SD	DK
11.	Have used information gained through Service-Learning to make changes in educational plans	SA	A	D	SD	DK
12.	Have used information gained through Service-Learning to make changes in career plans	SA	A	D	SD	DK
13.	Have shown increased advocacy for people, the community, or the environment	SA	A	D	SD	DK
14.	Have discovered or developed leadership skills	SA	A	D	SD	DK
15.	Are more able to work cooperatively in a group	SA	A	D	SD	DK
16.	Have become more involved in extracurricular activities	SA	A	D	SD	DK
17.	Have a better understanding of how school learning relates to future work and lifestyles	SA	A	D	SD	DK

These next questions are a little more demanding than the first ones, because here we're asking for examples, too. If you can't think of one right off, don't worry about it.

Has your involvement with Service-Learning . . .

18. Reinvigorated your teaching?
    Yes   No
    Example:

19. Energized your teaching strategies?
    Yes   No
    Example:

20. Motivated your students to learn?
    Yes   No
    Example:

*Adapted by Dr. Steve Cramer, University of Georgia, from material originated by the Florida State Department of Education.

21. Brought you respect and recognition from your colleagues and/or the community?
    Yes   No
    Example:

22. Helped you make student learning more relevant through world of work and service experiences?
    Yes   No
    Example:

23. Allowed you to observe increased self-esteem in your students?
    Yes   No
    Example:

24. As a teacher working with Service-Learning, in which of these areas do you feel you need assistance?
    _____ student recruitment
    _____ infusion of Service-Learning into the curriculum
    _____ infusion into club activities
    _____ reflection techniques
    _____ celebration ideas

Thank you for your feedback.

Wilkes County (Georgia)
Writing Sample Assessment Checklist Terminology
Kindergarten

CONTENT

Orally Describes Picture Drawn—Child tells what he/she has drawn. (Teacher writes what student says on the student's paper.)

Picture Story Relates to Topic—Picture drawn matches topic given and matches oral description given by student and written by teacher on child's paper.

Scribble with Picture—Contains few or no identifiable letters.

Script with Picture—Identifiable letters accompany picture; However, letters do not represent phonemic spellings.

Phonetic Representations of Words with Picture or Topic—Child's writing includes phonemic spellings about the picture or topic (i.e., initial, medical, and final consonants from appropriate words about the picture or topic).

Sentence Attempted about the Picture or Topic—Letters may be strung together in sentence form, may include phonemic spellings or words, and include a period at the end and possibly a capital at the beginning.

Identifiable Words or Sentences about the Picture or Topic—Word or words in sentences are identifiable.

GRAMMAR/MECHANICS

Beginning Sentence Capital Letters—Child uses capital letters at the beginning of complete sentences showing knowledge of the concept of capitalization. Sentences ended with periods; sentences begun with lower case "and" and then the word "I" are not sentences begun with a capital letter.

Punctuation (Sentence Ending Marks)—Child uses periods (and other appropriate ending marks) after complete sentences.

Inventive Spelling—Child uses inventive spelling for words not usually written by the average kindergartner. If no inventive spelling is present, mark a zero.

PENMANSHIP

Correct Formation of Letters and/or Numbers about Picture or Topic—Letters and numbers about the picture or topic are correctly formed.

Marking Scale—Assign a "0," or "1," only to the paper you are assessing. Do not decide if it's "yes" or "no" based on how the child has progressed, or what the child is doing in your classroom.

Developmental Stage—Determine the developmental stage. Use the description of stages on the attached sheet. Put the month and year next to the stage (e.g., Stage 1 9/xx).

Wilkes County
Kindergarten Writing Sample Assessment Checklist

Directions: Use the following Writing Benchmarks to assess the September & May writing assessment samples. Put a 0 or 1 in each block. Remember, these benchmarks reflect what a kindergarten student should be able to do at the end of the year.

Student Name _____ Teacher _____ Year _____

Writing Topic: **Narrative Essay**	September	May
CONTENT Orally Describes Picture Drawn		
Picture Story Relates to Topic		
Scribble with Picture		
Script with Picture		
Phonetic Representations of Words with Picture or Topic		
Sentence(s) Attempted about Picture or Topic		
Descriptive Words/Sentences about the Picture		
GRAMMAR/MECHANICS Beginning Sentence Capital Letters		
Sentence Ending Marks		
Inventive Spelling		
PENMANSHIP Correct Formation of Letters and/or Numbers about Picture or Topic		
TOTAL		

Marking Scale: 0 No   1 Yes

Developmental Stage (See attached sheet for description of each stage and page 67.)

Stage 1 _____   Stage 2 _____   Stage 3 _____   Stage 4 _____   Stage 5 _____   Stage 6 _____

September Total _____   May Total _____   IMPROVEMENT   NO IMPROVEMENT
                                                              (Circle One)

Comments:

_____

_____

_____

_____

Wilkes County (Georgia)
Writing Sample Assessment Checklist Terminology
First Grade

CONTENT
Picture Relates to Topic—Picture drawn matches topic given.

Appropriate Title—Title matches topic given, is separate from story, is clearly identifiable as a title, and is the actual name given to the story.

Words Relate to Topic—Individual words child has written relate to topic.
Sentence(s) Relate to Topic—Sentence(s) child has written relate(s) to topic.

STYLE
Uses Descriptive Words—Uses adjectives in the story.

GRAMMAR/MECHANICS
Punctuation (sentence ending marks)—Child uses periods and other appropriate ending marks, clearly exhibiting understanding of the use of sentence ending marks.

Beginning Sentence with Capital Letters—Child uses capital letters at the beginning of complete sentences, showing knowledge of capitalization. Sentences ended with periods, sentences begun with lower case "and," and then the word "I," are not sentences begun with a capital letter.

Complete Sentences—Child writes sentences that include a subject, verb, and object, beginning capital letter, and correct ending punctuation.

Correct Spelling of Basic Sight Words—Child spells basic sight words common to first graders. If child spells any basic sight word correctly (even only two or three), a "1" must be recorded.

Inventive Spelling—Child uses inventive spelling of words not usually written by the average first grader. If no inventive spelling is present, a "0" must be recorded.

PENMANSHIP
Correctly Formed Letters—Letters in words written about the picture or topic are correctly formed.

Correct Spacing between Letters and Words—Child uses correct spacing between the letters in words and correct spacing between the words.

Marking Scale—Assign a "0," "1," or "2" only to the paper you are assessing. Do not decide if it's "yes," "sometimes," or "no" based on how the child has progressed, or what the child is doing in your classroom.

Developmental Stage—Determine the developmental stage. Use the description of stages on the attached sheet. Put the month and year next to the stage (e.g., Stage 1 9/xx).

Wilkes County (Georgia)
Grade One Writing Sample Assessment Checklist

Directions: Use the following Writing Benchmarks to assess the September & May writing assessment samples. Put a 0, 1, or 2 in each block. Remember, these benchmarks reflect what a first-grade student should be able to do at the end of the year.

Student Name _____ Teacher _____ Year _____

Writing Topic: **Narrative Essay**	September	May
CONTENT Picture Relates to Topic		
Appropriate Title		
Words Relate to Topic		
Sentences Relate to Topic		
STYLE Uses Descriptive Words		
GRAMMAR/MECHANICS Punctuation (sentence ending marks)		
Beginning Sentence Capital Letters		
Complete Sentences		
Correct Spelling of Basic Sight Words		
Inventive Spelling		
PENMANSHIP Correctly Formed Letters		
Correct Spacing between Letters and Words		
TOTAL		

Marking Scale: 0 No, Never   1 Sometimes   2 Most of the Time

Developmental Stages (See attached sheet for description of each stage and page 67.)

Stage 1 ____   Stage 2 ____   Stage 3 ____   Stage 4 ____   Stage 5 ____   Stage 6 ____

September Total ____   May Total ____   IMPROVEMENT   NO IMPROVEMENT
                                                          (Circle One)

Comments:

_____

_____

_____

_____

Index

About the Author

David A. Payne received a bachelor's degree in psychology from Hope College (Holland, Michigan). After receiving a master's and doctor's degree from Michigan State University, he taught educational measurement and statistics for seven years at Syracuse University. He is currently director of test scoring and reporting services and professor of educational psychology at the University of Georgia. He teaches courses in program evaluation, educational assessment, and attitude scaling. Payne has published more than one hundred journal articles and book chapters and presented fifty papers at professional meetings. His most recent books are *Applied Educational Assessment* (Wadsworth), *Designing Educational Project and Program Evaluations* (Kluwer), and *Measuring and Evaluating Educational Outcomes* (Merrill).